Bloomsbury CPD Library: Senior Leadership

Jon Tait

BLOOMSBURY EDUCATION

LONDON OXFORD NEW YORK NEW DELHI SYDNEY

Bloomsbury Education
Bloomsbury Publishing Plc
50 Bedford Square, London, WC1B 3DP, UK

BLOOMSBURY, BLOOMSBURY EDUCATION and the Diana logo are trademarks of
Bloomsbury Publishing Plc

First published in Great Britain 2018

A catalogue record for this book is available from the British Library.

ISBN: PB: 978-1-4729-4538-9; ePDF: 978-1-4729-4537-2; ePub: 978-1-4729-4535-8

2 4 6 8 10 9 7 5 3 1 (paperback)

Typeset by Integra Software Services Pvt. Ltd.
Printed and bound by CPI Group (UK) Ltd, Croydon CR0 4YY

All papers used by Bloomsbury Publishing Plc are natural, recyclable products
from wood grown in well-managed forests. The manufacturing processes
conform to the environmental regulations of the country of origin.

To find out more about our authors and books visit www.bloomsbury.com and
sign up for our newsletters.

Contents

Contents

Acknowledgements

For years I have been watching great leaders – those I have been lucky enough to work with and be inspired by and those in the public eye whom I have never met but who have had an impact on me from afar. It is from these people – colleagues, line managers, role models and icons – that I have tried to take little bits, to piece together my own style of leadership. Whether it has been a senior leader who has inspired me to want to have a greater impact than just inside the four walls of my classroom, a sports coach delivering an inspirational team talk, or a state leader giving an inspiring battle cry to the nation that has modelled how to inspire action in others, I have always been fascinated by the way these highly-skilled professionals are agents for change.

However, we all need an opportunity to lead and develop as a leader in our own right and put these skills into practice. I am eternally grateful to all the leaders above me who saw enough in me to push me towards and, in some cases, to open up the door of opportunity for me at the various stages of my career. These people understood that leadership is not about creating followers, but about creating more leaders.

To those whom I've had the pleasure of working with, who have inspired me and given me the confidence to lead, I thank you. To those whom I've never met, but have inspired me to want to be like them, even in the smallest of ways, you'll never get to understand the impact you've had on me personally and the young people in my care.

And finally, to my wife Tracy. Without her support and belief in me, I would not have had the confidence and conviction to climb half the professional mountains that I have. When you have the love and support of someone to wake up to and go home to, even the most difficult situations and complex circumstances seem that little bit easier to overcome.

Introduction

This book is written from my personal experience of being a senior leader in two diverse and dynamic secondary schools, leading school improvement in many areas. The skills I have picked up from watching and working with others, and the experience this has given me to raise standards and the life chances of the young people in our care, are laid out for you in the forthcoming chapters.

Like a lot of professions, promotion in education means that, strangely, the better you get, the more you move away from what you are good at…teaching children. Senior leadership requires a very different skillset from the skills that have got you to where you are today. In most cases, senior leadership is about leading, motivating, monitoring and managing teachers. None of these skills are taught in your teacher training programme, so like most people, you will have picked up these skills and learned them 'on the job'. Ask lots of senior leaders and they'll probably tell you that they haven't had a lot of specific senior leadership training and anything they've had pales into insignificance compared to the training they received in their teacher training year. However, as we'll discover in the forthcoming chapters, leadership is the key to school improvement, so we should be investing more time in high-quality professional development for our current and aspiring leaders.

Put simply, great teachers don't always make great senior leaders. And certainly, great teachers without any specific attention to the skills they will need to lead a school will not make great senior leaders. Leadership is a craft of its own, just as teaching is, and it takes time and practice to get it right. There is also such a diverse range of leadership opportunities in most schools that some skills are very specific to some roles. Even if you've been a senior leader responsible for one area of school improvement, the chances are you'll need to learn a different set of skills to be successful in leading a different area of school improvement.

There are, however, leadership lessons that we can learn from outside of education. Great leaders know how to get the best out of the people in their organisations, irrespective of the context they are working in. Education is no different from any other profession in this respect. For years I used to coach

American football and was lucky enough to coach for Great Britain. The leadership skills that I learned in the school setting were easily transferable to the coaching field – vision, organisation, motivation and personal accountability. We should therefore be open to learning from great leaders not only within our profession, but outside of it too. Watching a great leader at work, either on the television or in a business or service that you come into contact with in your personal life, can be a model of excellence for you to aspire to. However, you have to be looking through the right lenses to spot the intricate detail that makes them great. The naked or uneducated eye will miss the vast majority of things that are happening, but if you watch though a leadership lens, you'll begin to spot the things that others don't.

This book will guide you through the initial steps to becoming a great senior leader, from applying and obtaining your first role, to enabling you to flourish in that role when you get there by providing you with the advice and training you'll need in a range of school improvement areas.

How to use this book

The Bloomsbury CPD Library provides primary and secondary teachers with affordable, comprehensive and accessible 'do-it-yourself' continuing professional development. This book focuses on becoming a senior leader.

The book is split into two halves: **Part 1 Teach yourself** and **Part 2 Train others**.

Part 1: Teach yourself

The first half of the book can be used according to where you are on your journey, either towards being a senior leader or in your quest to be the best senior leader that you can be.

- You may just be considering becoming a senior leader and use the book to gain an idea of the different and diverse roles in senior leadership.
- You could be using this book as a tool to help you understand your strengths and plug any gaps you have, readying yourself before applying for your first senior leadership position.
- You may have seen what you feel is the perfect senior leadership role to apply for and are using this book to help prepare your application and build your confidence (ahead of a possible interview) by having a full and proper understanding of senior leadership.
- You may have just been successful at interview for your first senior leadership post and are using this book to help you in your first steps in your new role.
- You may be facing challenges in your current senior leadership role and need some advice in how to remove the barriers that are blocking your road to success.
- Finally, you may be an experienced senior leader in one specific area and are looking to gain knowledge, advice and experience to widen your knowledge base to become a more well-rounded senior leader.

The first part of the book is split into five stages:

- **Stage 1 – Prepare:** Self-assessment, what are the different pathways, where do I see my career going and how can I best prepare for the role?

- **Stage 2 – Apply and obtain:** Planning your application and preparing for interviews.
- **Stage 3 – First steps:** Hitting the ground running in your new school.
- **Stage 4 – Leading:** Leading school improvement from the front.
- **Stage 5 – Enjoying senior leadership:** Not standing still in a dynamic educational landscape.

This comprehensive self-teach guide also includes teaching tips, 'to do' lists at the end of each chapter and recommendations for how you can share your ideas and practice with colleagues in your school and beyond. Further reading recommendations or titles to discuss in a CPD reading group are also included, as well as blog posts in bloggers' corner.

Part 2: Train others

Once you have become an experienced senior leader, it's time to help train other aspiring senior leaders or support new ones in areas that you excel in. This can be either in your own school as part of a leadership CPD pathway, or delivered externally with a group of local schools as part of a targeted leadership development programme for aspiring senior leaders. Whether it's a one-off session or part of a sustained leadership development programme, there are lots of session plans here to get you started. This section includes:

- Advice for delivering high-quality leadership development sessions.

- A full set of training plans covering the areas discussed in Part 1, including:
  o What's the right role for you?
  o Developing your vision for school improvement
  o Developing a personal action plan
  o Understanding the context of a school
  o Building relationships
  o Running effective meetings
  o Leading difficult conversations
  o Successful staff recruitment
  o Thinking about staff wellbeing
  o Developing teachers into expert practitioners
  o Creating digital networks for professional learning
  o Holding people to account
  o Planning and delivering an effective professional development day
  o Planning a conference and commercialising it
  o Planning a TeachMeet
  o Using a flipped learning approach to your professional development delivery
  o Creating video content for a flipped learning approach to professional development.

Online resources

For templates, questionnaires and PowerPoints from the book please visit:
www.bloomsbury.com/CPD-library-senior-leadership

Part 1

Teach yourself

STAGE 1: PREPARE: ARE YOU READY FOR SENIOR LEADERSHIP?

1

Are you ready?

The first step in your journey to senior leadership is to reflect on where you currently are and where you see yourself going. The first few chapters in this book will help you to reflect on your own skillset, whilst identifying the route you'd like to take on your journey to, and through, senior leadership.

This chapter is very different from the other chapters in the book as it is aimed at helping you be honest with yourself about your current strengths and gaps that you need to plug. Being honest with yourself about how well you are performing and where your gaps are can be easier said than done. Often when looking at yourself, it is difficult to see things objectively. Think of this self-assessment tool as a safe place where you can be at your most open and honest because nobody else is judging you.

How to complete the self-evaluation questionnaire

Following this introduction there is a questionnaire that you can complete as a self-assessment tool. This will give you an opportunity to think about senior leadership and help you form a clear view on where you are now and what the next steps will be for you personally. Depending on your own character and personal preference, there are three different approaches that you can take when answering these self-assessment questions:

Quick response approach

If your preference for the self-evaluation is to go with your gut only, then simply fill in the quick response section after each question with the first thing that comes into your mind when you ask yourself the question. Do not mull over the question too much, simply read carefully and answer quickly. This approach will give you an overview of your current understanding and practice in senior leadership and will take relatively little time. Just make sure you are uninterrupted, in a quiet place and able to complete the questionnaire in one sitting with no distractions, so that you get focused and honest answers.

Considered response approach

If you choose to take a more reflective and detailed approach, then you can leave the quick response section blank and go straight on to reading the further guidance section under each question. This guidance provides prompt questions and ideas to get you thinking in detail about the question being answered and is designed to open up a wider scope in your answer. It will also enable you to look at your experience and pull examples into your answer to back up your statements. You may want to complete it a few questions at a time and take breaks, or you may be prepared to simply sit and work through the questions all in one sitting to ensure you remain focused. This approach does take longer, but you will gain much more from the process than the quick response alone.

Combined approach

A thorough approach, and one I recommend, would be to use both approaches together regardless of personal preference. There is clear value in both approaches being used together. This would involve you firstly answering the self-evaluation quick response questions by briefly noting down your instinctual answers for all questions. The next step would be to return to the start of the self-evaluation, read the further guidance and then answer the questions once more, slowly and in detail, forming more of a narrative around each question and pulling in examples from your own experience. Following this, you would need to read over both

• I have done this self-assessment before. • I only want a surface-level overview of my current understanding and practice. • I work better when I work at speed. • I don't have much time.	**Quick**

• I have never done this self-assessment before. • I want a deeper understanding of my current understanding and practice. • I work better when I take my time and really think things over. • I have some time to do this self-assessment.	**Considered**

• I have never done this self-assessment before. • I have done this self-assessment before. • I want a comprehensive and full understanding of my current understanding and practice and want to compare that to what I thought before taking the self-assessment. • I have a decent amount of time to dedicate to completing this self-assessment.	**Combined**

Fig. 1 How should I approach the self-evaluation questionnaire?

responses and form a comprehensive and honest summary in your mind of your answers and a final view of where you feel you stand right now as a senior leader.

This is the longest of the three approaches to the questionnaire but will give you a comprehensive and full understanding of your current practice, thoughts and feelings in relation to senior leadership. You will be surprised at the difference you see between the quick response and the considered response answers to the same questions. It can be very illuminating.

Rate yourself

The final part of the self-evaluation is to rate yourself. This section will ask you to rate your confidence and happiness in each area that has been covered in the questionnaire, with a view to working on these areas for improvement throughout the course of the book. The table below shows how the scale works: the higher the number you allocate yourself, the better you feel you are performing in that area.

Rating	Definition
1	Not at all. I don't. None at all. Not happy. Not confident at all.
2	Rarely. Barely. Very little. Very unconfident.
3	Not often at all. Not much. Quite unconfident.
4	Not particularly. Not really. Not a lot. Mildly unconfident.
5	Neutral. Unsure. Don't know. Indifferent.
6	Sometimes. At times. Moderately. A little bit. Mildly confident.
7	Quite often. A fair bit. Some. A little confident.
8	Most of the time. More often than not. Quite a lot. Quite confident.
9	The majority of the time. A lot. Very confident.
10	Completely. Very much so. A huge amount. Extremely happy. Extremely confident.

Fig. 2 Rate yourself definitions

Top tip

Self-assessment is a vital skill for self-reflection and progression in your professional life. It is important that we are honest, kind and constructive when it comes to self-assessing. It can be easy to be too harsh on yourself when you self-assess and allow your insecurities to cloud your judgement. Being objective and honest about yourself and your practice is a hard thing to do and it takes practice. Before you begin self-assessing, it is important to carefully consider the criteria you are using to assess yourself and focus on those at first, without thinking about yourself. Feeling comfortable with what you are assessing will lead to a more accurate assessment. If you jump in and self-assess too early, before you have considered the assessment criteria, you may well have a clouded judgement and be unable to learn as much from the process. Don't rush it – it is too important.

Senior leadership self-evaluation questionnaire

QUESTION 1: What is the difference between leadership and management?

Quick response:

_____

_____

_____

_____

Questions for consideration

- Is there a difference between leadership and management?
- Can you describe roles in your school that might fit into these categories?
- Why do some roles fit into one category, but not the other?
- How might leadership and management styles differ depending on the context of a school?

Considered response:

_____

_____

_____

_____

_____

_____

_____

Rate yourself

QUESTION 1: On a daily basis, how often do you lead staff, rather than just manage them?

| 1 | 2 | 3 | 4 | 5 | 6 | 7 | 8 | 9 | 10 |

QUESTION 2: What makes a good leader?

Quick response:

_____

_____

_____

_____

Questions for consideration

- What qualities do you think a good leader needs to possess?
- How many of these qualities do you have?
- Which qualities do you need to develop?
- How could you develop these areas?

Considered response:

_____

_____

_____

_____

_____

_____

_____

_____

_____

_____

_____

_____

Rate yourself

QUESTION 2: How good a leader are you right now?

1	2	3	4	5	6	7	8	9	10

QUESTION 3: Which leader has inspired you and why?

Quick response:

_____

_____

_____

_____

Questions for consideration

- Have you worked with a leader that you really respected?
- What was it about them that inspired you?
- Outside of education, have any famous leaders inspired you?
- What qualities could you see in them that inspired you to want to be a leader?
- Have you worked with leaders who have not motivated you?
- Why was this?

Considered response:

_____

_____

_____

_____

_____

_____

_____

_____

_____

_____

_____

_____

Rate yourself

QUESTION 3: How inspiring are you as a leader?

1   2   3   4   5   6   7   8   9   10

QUESTION 4: Have you developed a sense of self-awareness of your own strengths and development points as a leader?

Quick response:

_____

_____

_____

_____

Questions for consideration

- What are your strengths?
- How did they become your strengths?
- Did you have to specifically work at any of these skills to make them your strengths?
- What are your development points?
- How can you improve these?
- Is there anyone in your school who has the exact skills that you need to improve on?
- Can you work with them to improve these areas?

Considered response:

_____

_____

_____

_____

_____

_____

_____

_____

Rate yourself

QUESTION 4: How self-aware are you of your current strengths and development points as a leader?

| 1 | 2 | 3 | 4 | 5 | 6 | 7 | 8 | 9 | 10 |

QUESTION 5: Have you a vision of what you'd like to achieve as a senior leader? And are you confident in being able to articulate this to staff?

Quick response:

_____

_____

_____

_____

Questions for consideration

- What is your educational ethos?
- How does your ethos match your current school's vision?
- Have you had experience of articulating a vision to staff before?
- Was this successful? Would you do anything differently next time?
- How might you get staff on board with a vision that may be reticent of change?

Considered response:

_____

_____

_____

_____

_____

_____

_____

_____

_____

_____

_____

Rate yourself

QUESTION 5: How clear is your vision?

1	2	3	4	5	6	7	8	9	10

QUESTION 6: How do you build relationships whilst motivating and inspiring staff to do their very best?

Quick response:

_____

_____

_____

_____

Questions for consideration

- What have you done to motivate staff in the past?
- Which methods have worked the best and why?
- Do those methods work for everyone?
- How are you going to motivate and inspire the harder-to-reach members of a staffroom?
- What quick wins can you achieve to make staff believe in you?

Considered response:

_____

_____

_____

_____

_____

_____

_____

_____

_____

Rate yourself

QUESTION 6: How confident are you in motivating a workforce to perform at their best, under the pressures that exist in today's schools?

| 1 | 2 | 3 | 4 | 5 | 6 | 7 | 8 | 9 | 10 |

QUESTION 7: Are you confident in holding others to account for their performance?

Quick response:

_____

_____

_____

_____

Questions for consideration

- Do all the staff under your responsibility understand the standards required and what is expected of them?
- Are you confident about having difficult conversations with staff, even if they are friends or long-term colleagues?
- Do you have a good knowledge of the procedures in place to deal with underperformance?
- Do you regularly praise staff for success and high performance?
- Have you had experience of leading the appraisal process with staff under your responsibility?

Considered response:

_____

_____

_____

_____

_____

_____

_____

Rate yourself

QUESTION 7: How confident are you in having difficult conversations with staff in order to hold people to account for their performance?

1   2   3   4   5   6   7   8   9   10

QUESTION 8: Do you have the personal drive to lead change and deliver continuous improvement in a school?

Quick response:

_____

_____

_____

_____

Questions for consideration

- How visible are you as a leader at the moment?
- Are you visible to students, staff, parents and governors?
- Do you have the drive and hunger for continuous school improvement, even if it gets tough?
- Can you positively influence others to help lead change?

Considered response:

_____

_____

_____

_____

_____

_____

_____

_____

_____

_____

Rate yourself

QUESTION 8: How committed are you to personally leading change and driving school improvement in schools where this may not have happened under previous leaders?

1   2   3   4   5   6   7   8   9   10

QUESTION 9: Are you confident in making tough decisions that may be unpopular but ultimately lead to school improvement?

Quick response:

_____
_____
_____
_____

Questions for consideration

- Have you had to make unpopular decisions before that have been in the best interest of the school or your department/faculty?
- How did you communicate the message so that it didn't cause staff unrest?
- What would you do differently next time?
- How might difficult messages need to be communicated to different audiences?
- Have you had experience of leading difficult meetings?
- What strategies did you use to ensure that you achieved what you wanted from the meeting?
- What can you learn from your experiences?

Considered response:

_____
_____
_____
_____
_____
_____
_____

Rate yourself

QUESTION 9: How confident are you in having to make unpopular decisions?

| 1 | 2 | 3 | 4 | 5 | 6 | 7 | 8 | 9 | 10 |

QUESTION 10: Have you developed a sense of emotional maturity so that you can deal with setbacks or criticism?

Quick response:

_____

_____

_____

_____

Questions for consideration

- Have you had any experience of when strategies you have put in place haven't gone so well?
- What can you learn from this?
- How do you keep sight of the bigger picture when faced with personal criticism?
- What do you do outside of school to refocus and maintain a sense of professional perspective?
- Are there any experiences in your life that you can draw on for emotional strength when faced with tough situations?

Considered response:

_____

_____

_____

_____

_____

_____

_____

Rate yourself

QUESTION 10: How confident are you in having to deal with personal setbacks and criticism, based on the decisions you make as a leader?

1   2   3   4   5   6   7   8   9   10

QUESTION 11: Are you able to create a climate of excellence for both staff and students where high expectations are the norm?

Quick response:

_____

_____

_____

_____

Questions for consideration

- Do you understand the expectations that your school requires from both its staff and students?
- How do you communicate this?
- How do you deal with situations when those expectations aren't met?
- Do you use different methods of dealing with underperformance in staff and students?
- Have you experienced situations where this hasn't been successful?
- What can you learn from this?

Considered response:

_____

_____

_____

_____

_____

_____

_____

_____

Rate yourself

QUESTION 11: Do you know what high expectations look like in all areas of school improvement?

1   2   3   4   5   6   7   8   9   10

QUESTION 12: How do you keep up to date with changes across the educational landscape?

Quick response:

_____

_____

_____

_____

Questions for consideration

- What mediums do you use to constantly keep learning?
- Which of these mediums are the most effective? Why is this?
- What do you need to learn more about?
- How can you do this?
- Do your current mediums enable you to do this, or do you need to source this information from elsewhere?

Considered response:

_____

_____

_____

_____

_____

_____

_____

_____

_____

Rate yourself

QUESTION 12: How often do you take time to learn and keep up to date with the changes in the educational landscape?

1	2	3	4	5	6	7	8	9	10

QUESTION 13: How effective are you at prioritising tasks and managing your own time?

Quick response:

_____

_____

_____

_____

Questions for consideration

- Have you developed your own systems for managing your own time?
- Are you able to prioritise important tasks over less important tasks?
- Do you stay late at school or take work home?
- How much time do you spend working at home?
- Are there staff you work with who seem to be very productive?
- What can you learn from these staff?

Considered response:

_____

_____

_____

_____

_____

_____

_____

_____

_____

_____

Rate yourself

QUESTION 13: How would you rate your own time-management skills?

| 1 | 2 | 3 | 4 | 5 | 6 | 7 | 8 | 9 | 10 |

QUESTION 14: Can you identify the aspects of teaching and school improvement strategies that make the most difference to student outcomes?

Quick response:

_____

_____

_____

_____

Questions for consideration

- Can you recognise good and outstanding teaching?
- How confident are you at coaching an experienced and competent member of staff to be even better?
- Have you got a track record of your action or development plans bringing about improved outcomes?
- What can you learn from the common characteristics of these strategies?
- Do you use published research to find out what makes the biggest difference to student outcomes?
- What have you found to be the best strategies that you have used in a classroom, or that your school has used across a whole cohort?
- Could any of these strategies be used in a different setting or a school in a different context?
- Why might this be?

Considered response:

_____

_____

_____

_____

_____

Rate yourself

QUESTION 14: Are you confident in your ability to recognise what makes the biggest differences to raising achievement and school improvement?

| 1 | 2 | 3 | 4 | 5 | 6 | 7 | 8 | 9 | 10 |

The results

Take a look at how you rated your answers for each question in the questionnaire and compare your ratings with the chart below, which will guide you to taking the next steps towards developing as a senior leader.

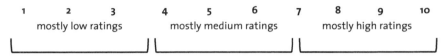

Fig. 3 How did you rate yourself?

Mostly low ratings

You have a way to go with your senior leadership but you are at the start of an exciting journey. Use this book as a guide to help you plug the gaps in your knowledge and experience so that you are in a position to begin applying for senior leadership roles in the near future. If you are already in a senior leadership role, but are looking for advice and further expertise, spend time observing other senior leaders you come into contact with and take time to reflect on what they do well.

Mostly medium ratings

You have begun to think carefully about senior leadership and are definitely ready to become a senior leader if you are not one already. Use this book to focus on the areas of senior leadership that you are not so confident about and look for opportunities in your current school to plug your gaps by broadening your work. It may be also time to seek shadowing opportunities in a different context to open your eyes to different approaches and styles of leadership.

Mostly high ratings

You have spent considerable time reflecting on your leadership and are developing strong skills as a senior leader. There are always areas that you can improve on and you are probably aware of what these areas are. You may be ready to coach and support other senior leaders who are less experienced or skilled than you. The training plans in Part 2 could be a very useful resource for you.

Now what?

The results are in. So now what? You have a full and detailed self-evaluation of your approach to being a senior leader and it is important that you now make the most of it. Take the time to put together an action plan based on the answers you have given and the conclusions you have drawn. Don't make this simply another bit of paperwork you have completed. Use it to really open your eyes to how far you have come, where you are now and what you want to do next. Prioritise what you want to work on and get going on it.

Chapter 1 takeaway

Teaching tip
As teachers we are often far too critical of ourselves when we are self-assessing. We tend to focus on what we think we need to do better and don't give equal time to congratulating ourselves on what we do well. Think about the difference you have made and the impact it has had on raising standards and school improvement.

Pass it on
Once you start reading about senior leadership and developing your own characteristics and skills, it is likely that you may want to talk about this with others. How you do this is up to you. You may want to discuss things verbally with a fellow colleague in your own school, or with a total stranger on social media as part of a professional learning network that you have developed. Either way, reflecting on your thoughts, experiences and challenges with other likeminded leaders will help you access advice when needed and see leadership through different lenses.

CPD book club recommendation
Teacher Toolkit by Ross Morrison McGill
(See bibliography)

Bloggers' corner
'What makes a great school leader?' by Elena Aguilar
Twitter handle: @artofcoaching1
(Link in bibliography)

TO DO LIST:

- [ ] Leave a little time after completing the questionnaire and then reread your answers and take time to reflect on what they reveal.
- [ ] Consider any area that you would like to work on that has been identified by your questionnaire.
- [ ] Begin to think about existing opportunities that you can utilise to start plugging some of those gaps.
- [ ] Read *Teacher Toolkit* by Ross Morrison McGill.
- [ ] Read 'What makes a great school leader?' by Elena Aguilar.

2 Senior leadership roles

Hopefully you are reading this book on the back of a successful career to date, working up from day-to-day classroom teaching into middle management, and after several successful years with a clear record of impact behind you, you feel the time is right to move into a senior leadership position. In my experience of doing just that, I have felt that the opportunity to lead a school has given me the greatest pleasure and personal satisfaction due to the much wider and significant impact that you can have on a group of young people. As a successful classroom teacher you only have an impact on 30 students at any given time, whereas as a school leader the changes and strategies that you put in place can benefit the whole school, thus your impact can be felt and seen so much more widely.

Have a vision

The other significant difference in moving into senior leadership is the need for vision. In most schools, middle leaders are the backbone of an organisation, but they are there to manage the school policies, ensuring compliance and the smooth running of the day-to-day operations. It is the senior leadership team that have the licence to be creative in determining the direction in which the school will travel, setting out their vision for constant school improvement and leading the school on its journey towards it. This can be daunting for some and exciting for others. The knowledge that you have a blank canvas in some schools to lay down your vision, tear up procedures that have become stale and use innovative approaches to bring about whole-scale change is not for everyone. But for those of us who get excited by this prospect of taking a key role in moving a school forward and having a significant role in improving the life chances of a generation of a whole community, then senior leadership is your ticket to complete job satisfaction.

Planning your route

Now you've decided to read on, in the knowledge that this is your calling in education, the first stage in your journey into senior leadership is to decide which direction you want to go in. You will no doubt have picked up various leadership skills, characteristics and credentials along the way through your career to date, but hopefully you're realistic enough to know that you don't possess the whole package right now. This is important to reflect on when looking at the area of senior leadership that you'd like to move into. A great starting point for career progression would be to move into a role that you are either really interested in or in which you have gathered significant skills and experience throughout your middle management roles.

The best way to look at the types of roles and areas of senior leadership that are generally on offer in most schools is to look at how schools are held to account. Due to the latest Ofsted framework splitting the work of schools into four main distinct areas (plus early years provision or 16–19 study programmes if applicable), many schools now focus on these areas as overall areas of leadership responsibility, thus making it easier for people in the organisation to be held accountable for the performance of these areas.

Ofsted currently split the overall effectiveness of a school into the following four main areas:

1. Effectiveness of leadership and management.
2. Quality of teaching, learning and assessment.
3. Personal development, behaviour and welfare.
4. Outcomes for pupils.

Within each of these areas there are a wide range of roles and responsibilities. Each school will have a slightly different hierarchical leadership structure depending on size and context, but all will have a leadership structure in place to ensure the effectiveness of all four areas. In larger schools this may mean that specific and distinct roles are created under only one of the four areas, whereas in smaller schools with smaller teams, roles may encompass more than one of the four areas. Consideration must therefore be given to whether you apply for a role in a large school with a possible smaller focus in terms of Ofsted areas, or a smaller school with fewer students and staff, but with a possible wider range of responsibility areas.

The structure of senior leadership

Most schools operate with a three-level structure at senior leadership.

Assistant headteacher

Assistant headship is the first level in this model where leaders have distinct roles and responsibilities, usually relating to one of the four main Ofsted areas. Depending on the size and context of a school, you may find numerous assistant headteachers operating in one senior leadership team. This is the level that most people progress into from middle management.

Deputy headteacher

The next level up usually comprises a deputy headteacher, or more than one in big schools. Although in some cases people can transition from middle leadership straight into deputy headship (this is usually dependant on the context and size of the school, together with the experience of the individual), it is normally seen as a stepping stone upwards for assistant headteachers once they have had experience of successfully leading a school at that level.

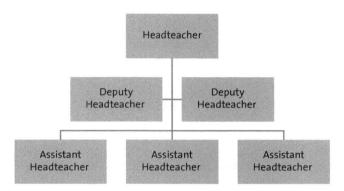

Fig. 4 Typical senior leadership staffing structure

Headteacher

Finally, the third level is principal, headteacher or executive headteacher, depending on the size and context of the school. Although there is not a written rule, especially now that the NPQH qualification is no longer an essential requisite for headteachers, professionals at this level normally come from having worked at the deputy headteacher level in a school previously. However, there have been moves in some parts of the country to look at appointing highly successful leaders and CEOs of organisations outside of education to fill the voids that some schools find.

This chapter will help you understand the variety of senior leadership roles on offer in most schools and aid you in determining the direction you'd like your career to go in. Having read this chapter, you should be able to decode the sometimes fancy job titles in the *TES*, understanding more about what the roles might entail and whether they are worth considering, based on your chosen career path.

We're now going to break down the four Ofsted areas, looking at the types of roles and responsibilities that most schools require in order to gain the very best judgement for overall effectiveness and, in turn, provide the very best value to all of their key stakeholders.

Effectiveness of leadership and management

It is important to remember that the most important factor in any organisational improvement strategy is leadership. This is the same inside and outside of education. If strong leadership, together with a clear and articulated vision, isn't present at the top of the organisation, people can be working as hard as they want underneath, but never getting anywhere due to a lack of strategic focus and direction.

The overall responsibility of leadership and management that runs throughout all of the other areas that we will talk about is holding people to account. This is essential to high performance and is a common characteristic of any successful leader or successful organisation. At leadership level you must be able to put any friendship or personal relationship aside and hold people to account for what they are being paid to deliver on. This can be tough if you have worked your way up through one school and are now being asked to have difficult conversations about staff performance with people you have sat shoulder to shoulder with in the staffroom for years, but that is the role of a leader. If you have children yourself, always think about whether the standard of performance, either in an individual teacher or throughout the whole school, would be good enough for your own children.

Although you are tasked with holding people to account, you will only get the very best out of people if you can motivate and inspire them. People will only work so hard for you out of fear; the extra ten per cent comes from their respect for you and the fact that you have motivated and inspired them to do their very best. Inspiration can come in many forms, but in my experience it comes from having integrity as a leader, understanding your staff as human beings, not just as employees, and enthusiastically articulating your vision, starting with the why. People are always more likely to get behind or on board with a strategy if they know and understand why it is happening. Far too often in underperforming schools, decisions are taken and procedures and policies put in place without sharing the why with the people on the ground. In these circumstances you will find a staffroom of voices moaning about the constant things they have to do that seem pointless.

Now that we understand that holding people to account, whilst motivating and inspiring staff, is a golden thread that runs throughout every senior leadership role, let us look more specifically at some of the distinct roles and responsibilities that may fall under the area of effective leadership and management.

- **Staff appraisal** – Conducting staff appraisal throughout the year, ensuring individual teachers and responsibility holders are held to account for their classroom performance and their own professional development.
- **Staffing and human resources** – Staff performance reviews, creating, delivering and monitoring informal and formal capability plans, development of staffing structures that meet the needs of the curriculum, consulting and meeting with union representatives on policy changes that will affect staff working practices or staff numbers, covering staff who are absent with high-quality short- and medium-term replacements.
- **Recruitment and retention** – Advertising for new roles, recruitment of high-quality staff, retaining existing staff.
- **Quality assurance** – Monitoring the quality of educational provision across the whole school, holding middle leaders to account for the quality of provision in their department or faculty, reporting on the quality of provision to major stakeholders, developing action plans to address areas of development identified by quality assurance.
- **Budget and finance** – Responsibility for individual or whole-school spending via designated budgets, balancing budgets based on allocated income, delivering quality of provision that matches curriculum needs with allocated funds, sourcing extra streams of income or revenue, gaining best value for money, using current resources to the very best of their ability.
- **Governance** – Reporting the overall effectiveness of the school to governors, developing links for governors to meet with key senior staff to hold them to account for their areas of responsibility, ensuring that governors are an integral part of the leadership of the school and effectively holding senior leaders to account.

Quality of teaching, learning and assessment

Any school that wants a sustainable school improvement method must concentrate on getting the quality of teaching right in the classroom. A sticky-plaster-style intervention approach in the examination years (Year 6/ Year 11) is only a short-term fix and should only be used to supplement what is happening in the classroom. Any school that bases their school improvement strategies around a sticky-plaster-style approach will only end up burning out staff and heaping too much stress on their students at the most important time in their education. It also begs the question of what is actually happening day in and day out in your classrooms if you are having to spend so much time, money and energy on last-minute intervention.

Teaching and learning should ultimately trump everything else in school. It should be at the heart of school improvement as it is our core business. Senior leaders should be constantly striving for the very best provision in the classrooms of their schools every single minute of every single day. However, in the dynamic educational landscape that we operate in, we must provide cutting-edge input and support so that our staff are leaders and experts in their specialist fields. This must be underpinned by highly bespoke and differentiated professional development programmes that inspire, challenge and truly develop the talented professionals that we put in front of our children every day.

These are some specific roles and responsibilities that may fall under this area:

- **Assessing the quality of teaching** – Monitoring the quality of teaching through the school's quality assurance systems, analysing individual/ departmental/faculty/whole-school trends, developing action plans to improve on areas for development at individual/departmental/whole-school level, reporting on the quality of teaching to the major stakeholders.
- **Assessment** – Quality-assuring the rigour/validity/accuracy of assessments, analysis of data relating to assessment, ensuring rigour of moderation to increase the accuracy of assessment.
- **Professional development** – Planning and delivering high-quality and highly bespoke professional development, developing a culture of learning amongst your staff.
- **Professional coaching** – Supporting colleagues in small groups or one-to-one to improve their classroom performance, working with individual teachers on specific areas of classroom practice.
- **NQTs and ITT** – Planning and delivery of induction programmes, mentoring of individual members of staff, development and training of high-quality subject mentors, maintaining and developing further external links with teacher training agencies.

Personal development, behaviour and welfare

Most experts on school improvement will tell you that establishing high levels of student behaviour is the first thing that you should look to do when moving into a failing or struggling school. Without a collective positive attitude to learning from the student body, outcomes will never be as good as they could be. In an environment where this is the case, there is also usually a high turnover of teaching staff due to the lessons being constantly disrupted by poor behaviour. Therefore, getting this right as quickly as you can has multiple knock-on benefits to your school, not only in being able to increase student outcomes, but also to retain the best staff that you have at your disposal.

If there's one thing that can get your school closed almost overnight, it's a serious safeguarding breach. Over the past ten to 15 years, this has become the most important factor in any school across the land. A school inspection might not even get going if the inspection team notice a safeguarding issue when they arrive on site. Everything we do now as a school must revolve around the safeguarding of our young people and, as a senior leader for the pastoral side of the school under this area, you (under delegated responsibility from the headteacher) will probably be ultimately responsible for this.

Specific roles and responsibilities in this area might include:

- **Student behaviour** – Responsibility for improving whole-school behaviour, senior lead on fixed-term exclusions and permanent exclusions, identifying barriers to learning.
- **Rewards and sanctions** – Development and management of whole-school rewards and sanctions systems, analysis of trends relating to individual students/departments/whole school.
- **Alternative provision** – Sourcing suitable alternative provision for select individuals or groups of students, quality-assuring any alternative provision, ensuring the curriculum is fit for purpose and that students are making adequate progress, seeking best value for money for all alternative provision places based on the progress that students make.
- **Attendance and punctuality** – Ensuring students attend school every day, raising the attendance of students who are persistently absent, improving punctuality of school arrival, identifying barriers to attending school, working with families, prosecutions and fines.
- **Safeguarding** – Child protection, prevention of radicalisation, student welfare.
- **SMSC** – Planning for the delivery and promotion of activities and opportunities that enable students to develop spiritually, morally, socially and culturally, together with the promotion of British values.
- **Student leadership** – School council, student voice, student leadership opportunities.

Outcomes for pupils

At the end of the day, all of the three previous areas should, if carried out effectively, lead to improved student outcomes. Nobody will believe that the quality of teaching in your school is of a high standard if you have a poor track record of results. You also need to take into account that the outcomes that your students receive go a long way to determining the overall quality of your school. Put simply, outstanding outcomes usually lead to an outstanding Ofsted judgement.

However, this doesn't just happen by chance and the aggregated accumulation of good teaching and good behaviour. Lots of work is required to motivate students, track their progress and intervene when necessary. The work of a highly skilled senior leadership team in this area should not be seen just as a sticky-plaster approach, like I mentioned earlier in this chapter, but instead as the perfect partner to high-quality classroom teaching, pushing students to do their very best.

Roles and responsibility areas relating to outcomes for pupils might include:

- **Student outcomes** – Overall responsibility for student outcomes (both external examinations and internal assessments) and key performance indicators.
- **Data tracking** – Tracking of student attainment and progress data, closing gaps between sub-groups, analysis of trends relating to individual students/departments/whole school.
- **Reporting to parents** – Responsibility for the quality of written reports to parents, strategic lead on when and how the school reports to parents, together with what data the school reports home on, management of parents' evenings.
- **Intervention** – Coordination of intervention for students who have been identified as requiring further help to reach their targets.
- **Curriculum mapping** – Responsibility for mapping the curriculum to the needs of the students, together with guidance from the Department for Education (DfE).
- **Timetabling** – Ensuring the desired curriculum can be taught by the current number of staff available in the current number of classrooms available.

Chapter 2 takeaway

Teaching tip

The breadth and variety of the day-to-day work that a senior leadership team does is phenomenal. Taking the time to reflect on your previous experience and your passions will enable you to hopefully map out the path that you'd like to take. The rest of this book will not go into specific detail about any one of the four previous areas, but instead will look at the generic leadership skills that you will require in order to be successful. Whichever area you are more drawn to from the previous list, try to use the following chapters with that specific context in mind, putting yourself in that role.

Pass it on

Talk to colleagues in your school who are in different senior leadership positions. Ask them about their roles, what they like and dislike about them. Try to gain as much insight into the roles as you can from people who are currently performing them. Start to try to work out which area of senior leadership you'd like to specialise in.

CPD book club recommendation

The Best Job in the World by Vic Goddard
(See bibliography)

Bloggers' corner

'10 top tips for teachers heading into senior leadership teams' by Jill Berry
Twitter handle: @jillberry102
(Link in bibliography)

TO DO LIST:

- ☐ Reflect on the different areas of senior leadership and where your current skillset may lie.
- ☐ Think about the area of senior leadership you'd like to move into and compare this to your skillset. Is it the same?
- ☐ Think about highly skilled senior leaders whom you have worked with. What made them great?
- ☐ Read *The Best Job in the World* by Vic Goddard.
- ☐ Read '10 top tips for teachers heading into senior leadership roles' by Jill Berry.

3 Plugging your gaps

You've hopefully now had a good chance to think about your own readiness for senior leadership, together with looking at the full range and diversity of roles and responsibilities that are required in most schools. If you've skipped to this chapter and not had a chance to reflect on your own skillset and vision for leadership, or if you feel you need to do this in more depth, I would strongly recommend the following two steps.

Step 1: Identify and understand your gaps

Self-evaluation questionnaire

Take a look through the self-evaluation questionnaire in Chapter 1 and complete each question. Whilst answering each question, take the time to reflect on your previous experiences, whilst also thinking about your personal goals over the next few years. It is important that this is a completely honest reflection and is not swayed by pride or peer pressure. Only when you have an accurate picture of your readiness for the next step can you map out an action plan that will get you there.

Peer-evaluation

Although performing a self-evaluation is critical to identifying and understanding your areas for development, it is always important to ask how other people view you. This can sometimes be hard to hear, but it is worth its weight in gold. Our opinion of ourselves can sometimes be very different to the opinion that others have of us. Sometimes this can be because we doubt ourselves, have low confidence or are generally modest about our impact and influence; yet other times it can be due to an inflated self-confidence or an inaccurate barometer of what constitutes quality. Either way, having the courage to ask a trusted close circle of colleagues about your strengths and possible shortcomings can be one of the most important reflection activities you ever do.

If you decide on a peer-evaluation, there are lots of '360 leadership assessment' activities online that you can use, or alternatively you can create your own bespoke one by thinking about all of the areas that you'd like to be evaluated on, together with a quick and easy scoring system. The only stipulation that is required to make this as accurate as possible is to ask your colleagues to be brutally honest. It is no good just hearing what they think you want to hear. This needs to be a warts-and-all evaluation; otherwise it will not be any different to your own self-evaluation and therefore a waste of time and energy. This can be tricky though, depending on who you ask and what their professional or personal relationship is to you. My tip in ensuring this is as accurate as possible is to use an online tool that allows all evaluations to be anonymous so that the respondents can answer truthfully without the worry of potentially upsetting you.

Remember that you may find some of the feedback from your peers to be a little different from your own perception of yourself and this can be disappointing and even hurtful. However, you must remember that if this is how your colleagues truly view you, then you need to take this on board. They subconsciously observe you every day at work in some way or another, so their opinions are extremely important. At the end of the day, it is no good thinking you are good at something if everyone around you has a very different opinion.

Step 2: Plugging your gaps

Once you have a true and accurate picture of your current readiness for senior leadership from both your self- and peer-evaluation activities, you can look at how to plug any gaps you may have identified. Every person reading this book will be slightly different and this is understandable. It is fine to not be the finished article right now. It may be that the majority of your gaps are purely down to a lack of opportunity or experience, rather than it being a reflection of your own proficiency. Any gaps you have can be plugged in a range of different ways and, depending on your context, you may choose to use a range of the following methods. Some ways will be more appropriate for certain gaps and contexts than others.

Colleagues

There's a pretty good chance that there will be an expert in your school for every area that you need to work on. What you need to do to begin with is work out who they are. For most skills this may be relatively easy and you can probably identify them off the top of your head right now. These are the people whom you've worked with for a number of years and are maybe leaders whom you aspire to be like. However, some skills are a little less obvious to the naked eye and are not necessarily on show every day. These are the skills that you might need to ask your current headteacher or another senior colleague about. Your headteacher will know where these skills lie and should be able to identify colleagues for you to approach.

Once you have identified these colleagues, you then need to take the time to approach them and ask them if they are willing to help upskill you. To do this, don't catch somebody in the corridor when they are running to a meeting or on the way to a class; make some time to sit down with them at a time that works for you both. This way you can talk about why you are doing this and how important it is for you professionally, therefore probably gaining a much better response.

There are many ways in which these colleagues can help you plug your gaps. Firstly, they can try to train you in a specific area through one-to-one meetings that you arrange. The problem with this approach is that it is time-consuming to them. Taking a few hours out of an already busy week can sometimes not be possible. The second, and less time-intensive, way for the colleague is to ask if you can shadow them at some stage when they are involved in activities related to that skill. This might be in parental meetings, faculty meetings or even when analysing data or timetabling. This can also be the perfect way to witness these skills in a real-life situation, rather than in a false context like a training session. If you are lucky and have supportive colleagues, combining these two approaches will give you both the theory and the practice, enabling you to think about the skills and then see them in action.

Networking

As teachers, we usually know other teachers in the profession, or we know of friends of friends who are in similar positions. This has been made even easier in the past few years by the huge education movement on social networking sites such as Twitter and LinkedIn, where you can access support from like-minded professionals all over the world. Personally, I have found this to be the most effective form of advice, support and challenge that I have ever had. Growing my professional network of contacts to approaching 10,000 educators from across the globe has meant that I have been able to be inspired and reach out for inspiration whenever and wherever I have needed it.

This can also be a great way of being able to plug your gaps and receive help without broadcasting it to your current colleagues. Some of you may be in a context where this is difficult to talk about, or you want to go about this side of your development quietly, and this is fine. Like I mentioned earlier, everyone will be different. It also gives you the opportunity to compare and contrast your advice from different contexts, sometimes in different countries, enabling you to gain a much wider perspective on certain areas.

If you are interested in getting a professional network established online, a great place to start is a blog by Ross Morrison McGill – '10 tips for tweeting teachers' (link in bibliography).

School visits

Just like in our previous approach, organising to visit another school, where there is an area of excellence that you are looking to plug one of your gaps with, gives you the chance to view it in another context. One of the downsides of the first approach, where you source your development from your existing colleagues, is that you sometimes get brainwashed into one way of thinking (and this may not be good if your school isn't the highest performing of schools). Getting out to see a different school in action is always good development and in this case can open your eyes to new ways of leadership that you may not have been exposed to previously in your career.

Organising these visits can sometimes be tricky though. How do you find out where the strands of excellence that you are looking for are on display? In my experience, your local authority is usually a good source of knowledge. Even in this world of academisation and reduced local authority control, they will still usually know where the best practice lies and will have had plenty of contact with the most influential leaders. At worst, they can point you in the direction of the most successful headteachers, who can then delegate the task of your development to the right person in their team.

If you get the opportunity, try to find a school that is a little bit further away from home in a completely different location and context. Seeing how different schools operate and lead in areas such as inner cities, coastal towns and rural areas can vary hugely, due to the very nature of the different issues that come through their doors every day.

External courses

Sometimes if you haven't been able to source the experience from one of the above three approaches, you may feel it necessary to look at a specific external professional development course. The beauty of this is that you get the chance to be away from school and have the head space to truly learn and reflect on your own development. However, sometimes you can feel that some of the courses and presenters are a little bit removed from the reality of school life and that you could have got a more authentic experience with somebody who is presently doing that role.

Courses can also be very expensive, especially when you take into account the course cost plus travel and then cover implications. If you are looking to move on from your school into a senior leadership role at another school, you need to be mindful that in the current economic climate, you'll probably find that a lot of schools will be reluctant to pay for such a course if they know you are looking to feather your cap to enable you to leave.

Books

If you want to keep your development to yourself and don't want the expense or the hassle of external courses, the best method might be to read. Over the past ten years there has been a significant increase in the number of current practitioners who have written books on every subject from general classroom practice to leading failing schools. These authors bring significant authenticity to their writing because they are still in school doing what they are preaching, as opposed to some books that you feel are written with the best intentions, but without the understanding of how hard it is on the ground.

If you like reading, or you'd like to use this method to supplement one or two of the other approaches, check out the impressive list of Bloomsbury Education titles and the Bloomsbury CPD library. Being able to read in your own time and pick it up and put it down whenever you choose might be the perfect method for you during the next few months. With books, there's also the opportunity to revisit them at any time in the future when you need them.

Practice

Sometimes you might feel that you have the knowledge of the skills you need to develop; you just need more practice at them. If you are at this stage, then you need to seek out opportunities to practise and hone your craft. For example, it may be that you need more practice at difficult conversations. In this instance, although you don't want to create situations that require a difficult conversation, when the opportunity presents itself you need to grab it and not avoid it. Some of these opportunities will come your way in your day-to-day role, but some of them may need you to seek them out in the form of shadowing another colleague, like we talked about in the first approach.

It is also worth thinking about the fact that 'purposeful practice makes perfect'. When carrying out some of your tasks throughout the week, it's worth bearing this in mind and consciously trying to improve your skillset in leadership. Having this at the forefront of your mind means that you are not merely going through the motions, but always thinking about how you can be the best leader you can be, even if some of the things you are doing seem second nature to you.

Action plans

Now you've understood your gaps and hopefully identified some approaches that will help you plug them, it is well worth taking some time to commit yourself to an action plan. With the best will in the world we can all say that we are going to do something, but then the general day-to-day busy-ness of school takes over and, before we know it, we are at the weekend again. By forming a strategic action plan of what you are going to do, with whom, and to what timelines, you can hold yourself to account for your own development. It also tends to feel so much more manageable when you get your thoughts down on paper into small steps so you can see them. You'll also feel like you've achieved something just by putting your plan together. The next step is to check the points off your list or colour code them (RAG rate) as you make progress against your targets. This will keep you motivated so you can see how far you have come and how close you are getting to your ultimate goal of landing that first senior leadership post.

Chapter 3 takeaway

Teaching tip

Think about which approaches might work best, based on the gaps that you are trying to plug. You may find that you do not have the opportunity to utilise all of them and you may also find that some are more applicable than others. Remember that this list should not be seen as a list where you only have to select one approach. By using a range of approaches, you are going to create the very best environment and opportunities in which to plug your gaps in the most effective ways.

Pass it on

Use the colleagues you work with as a sounding board. Speak to them about helping you with your peer-evaluation, ask them for help in plugging your gaps and don't feel you need to make this journey on your own. You may also find that there is another colleague in your school who is also looking to develop their own skills. Why not work together to review each other's action plans and be a support for each other as you both move towards your respective professional goals?

CPD book club recommendation

8 Qualities of Successful School Leaders by Jeremy Sutcliffe
(See bibliography)

Bloggers' corner

'What should we look for in senior leaders?' by Stephen Tierney
Twitter handle: @LeadingLearner
(Link in bibliography)

TO DO LIST:

- ❑ Ensure you have completed your self- or peer-evaluation.
- ❑ Identify a range of different ways in which you can gain the experience, skills or practice to plug the gaps that you have identified.
- ❑ Draw up an action plan with timelines of when these opportunities will take place.
- ❑ Read *8 Qualities of Successful School Leaders* by Jeremy Sutcliffe.
- ❑ Read 'What should we look for in senior leaders?' by Stephen Tierney.

4 Picking the right school

Picking the right school is imperative at this stage of your career. A wrong move in the wrong direction and at the wrong time could make you wish you'd just stayed in the classroom. This decision shouldn't be taken lightly and you should endeavour to take your time in making a decision about where to apply and for which positions. After all, a school needs to be right for you, just as you need to be right for them. Your first senior leadership position will be hard enough as it is, without being in a school that is not the right fit for you and doesn't share the same values.

In most cases, teachers who have shown great promise as middle leaders and are looking for their first senior leadership job are not looking to jump ship straight away. I'm guessing that you have been successful in your role, have gained great experience and enjoy your school, so you are probably not looking to leave at the very first opportunity. Unless you are in a very different position, it is my recommendation to sit tight, keep your eyes open to the opportunities that might come up around you and then make the right move at the right time. Quick moves based on knee-jerk reactions can sometimes turn out to be bad moves that people regret later down the line. We all know the saying that 'the grass isn't always greener'.

However, you should not be afraid of change. Lots of teachers end up working in the same school for years and years, just because it is comfortable for them and it is what they have always known. As long as you take your time in making the right move at the right time, then you should have nothing to worry about. I hear lots of people say to me 'but I'll miss the kids'. Every school has students you'll bond with, laugh with and build relationships with; and the same goes for staff teams. What you leave behind in one building, you'll pick up in another.

Travelling distance

One of the biggest things to think about when looking at new opportunities is the travelling distance that a school is away from your home. This should be carefully calculated when you are weighing up whether a school is right for you. However, there are several schools of thought on this and there is no right or wrong answer; it is merely your preference.

A school close to home

Working at a school very close to home can bring many benefits in terms of extra time in bed in the morning and the ability to finish school and be home very quickly. The other benefit is the knowledge of local context that you may have in terms of communities, areas of the town and partner/feeder primary schools. However, the downsides include the fact that you might live in the same community as the students you teach. This can sometimes prove to be problematic, especially if you end up being in charge of behaviour or exclusions and constantly end up running into some of your more challenging families in the local community.

A school further away from home

Travelling a distance to school every day does not appeal to everyone. Although you are further away from your natural catchment area (as highlighted with the school close to home), you need to factor in how much time it will add on to your normal working day. You also need to take into consideration how much extra petrol or diesel will be required. Going for a promotion with a £2,000 to £3,000 pay rise may well be instantly wiped out due to increased fuel costs every day just getting there and back, and that is before you factor in the extra time on the road every day. However, lots of people say that a commute that isn't too long but is far away enough from home to give them some down time in the car is perfect. Having that 'me time' to reflect, think, relax or sing can be just what you need every day. Without this time, you can end up leaving the pressure of school and getting home within a few minutes to be possibly faced with the pressure of your own children, making tea, looking at homework, etc. In my experience a travel time of approximately 30 minutes has enabled me to be home from school fairly easily, but also gives me the perfect 'me time' to and from school every day.

Relocating

In some cases, you might find that you are prepared to move away if the right opportunity presents itself. This can be either in this country or further afield, with many international schools actively recruiting British teachers with the promise of a better quality of life on offer. Whichever location you choose, you need to ensure that the location is right for both you and your family (if applicable). The stress of a new role at a new school will only intensify if either you or your family don't settle in your new area. Take the time to do your research and homework on relocating if that is something you are seriously considering. A move like this should never be a knee-jerk reaction.

Types of schools

Aside from location, there are many other factors to consider when deciding if a school is right for you. Everything from the size and structure of the school to how they have performed in their last Ofsted and set of examination results should be considered. A smart professional who is about to make a potential career-defining decision should not go into this next stage with their eyes closed. One of the best ways to do this is to visit the school and try to get a feel for it as you walk round. Try to go when the school has children in it. Have your eyes and ears open and try to imagine yourself in that setting.

Your home school

For some, gaining a promotion in your current school might be the ideal situation. You already know the staff, the students and the context, so surely this will be an easier transition into the next phase of your career than having to start again somewhere else? However, being able to experience a different setting and context can make you far more considered in your approach to leadership, bringing experience of more than one ethos/approach to your strategies and solutions. It is also worth thinking about establishing yourself as a leader. Although you may feel that it might be hard to establish your reputation all over again in a new school, think about the relationships you have had with your colleagues over the years in your current school. Will these have to significantly change if you are now line-managing them? How are you going to change from the person whom they rubbed shoulders with over lunch or had a joke with in the staffroom, to the one who is now holding them to account for their performance through their appraisal? Sometimes establishing yourself as a leader in a new school can be a little easier.

Multi-academy trusts (MATs)

The introduction and rapid growth of MATs throughout the educational landscape over the last ten years has changed the face of education. Within these MATs, there may be significantly more opportunities for development and promotion opportunities across the trust and therefore the ability to work in more than one context. This appeals to lots of people who are eager to seek new opportunities or to have the ability to have an impact on more than one site, or in more than one context. However, there are possible drawbacks. If you are leading in a MAT school and your skillset is badly required in another of the MAT schools, there may be a possibility that you might be asked to go and work in that school for a period of time to up-skill a certain team. This might sound great to begin with, but some MATs have quite a large geographical footprint and suddenly the travelling distances, times and expense that we covered in the previous section may now start to become an issue.

'Inadequate' schools

Although every person reading this book will be different, you may find that starting your leadership journey in a school that is inadequate (either 'special measures' or 'serious weaknesses') may be a baptism of fire. With the introduction of MATs and the fact that the Secretary of State has a duty to make an academy order for all maintained schools and pupil referral units (PRUs) that are inadequate, it is highly likely that an established MAT will come in to sponsor an inadequate school shortly after an Ofsted inspection and bring in their own leadership to get the school back on track. It is therefore worth understanding the whole context of a school and whether this is really the right time and right place for you.

'Requires improvement' schools

In schools that Ofsted have rated as 'requires improvement', there are lots of opportunities to go in and make a difference. Although these schools are under pressure to improve, as long as the HMI inspector is confident that the leadership team have the capacity to make the improvements, then they will generally be left alone to put their action plans in place. In both the special measures and requires improvement categories of schools, leadership opportunities may present themselves because, by the very nature of the performance of the school under the previous leadership, things haven't been good enough. Many schools use this opportunity to create new roles and re-shuffle their teams, getting the right people on the bus, in the right seats and going in the right direction. Going into a school at this time can be a great opportunity to demonstrate your impact very quickly, and these schools are usually far more open to change and new, innovative approaches than schools that are already doing well.

'Good' schools

Good schools can be great to work in, due to the very nature of their performance rating from Ofsted, but should also be treated with caution. In some cases, where a school has just got to a good judgement after a tough journey from 'requires improvement', there can be a sense of unhappiness. Staff teams have literally given everything they can physically give to get their school out of 'requires improvement'. The teamwork and camaraderie during these times is what makes people tick and gets them through, only to be told when they finally reach the promised land that good is now not good enough – 'We're now pushing for outstanding'. The collective sigh of relief and time to relax, now that a team has got to good, disappears pretty quickly because, as we know, school improvement is relentless in the drive to outstanding. One thing to remember here is that the journey is sometimes more enjoyable than the destination.

'Outstanding' schools

Every school has pressures; they just come in different shapes and sizes. This is no different in an outstanding school. The pressure to maintain an outstanding status can be just as heavy as the pressures at the other end of the spectrum. Within these schools it is also worth considering that if they have a successful model that has got them to outstanding, they are going to be very reluctant to change it – 'If it ain't broke, don't try and fix it'. A model of 'compliance rather than creativity' may breed through the school, thwarting the more innovative and creative amongst us. These are usually not schools where you can go in with a blank canvas and start to make a quick and noticeable impact. However, you may feel that being in the same day-to-day environment and learning from a team of outstanding leaders is just what you are looking for in your first role in senior leadership.

'Start-up' schools

Some schools, like free schools, may be starting from a complete blank canvas as a brand new school. In these schools, the opportunity to help create a new school, from the policies to the paintwork, may excite many people, but also be daunting to others.

Do your research

Once you have considered the different options above and have started to look seriously at some opportunities that have been advertised, it is vital that you do your research on the school. In this day and age with the wonders of the internet, you can do your homework from the comfort of your own home. Everything you need to know to begin with you can find out within a few minutes. Try to piece together all the information that you can find on a school to see if it matches how they have marketed it to you in the advert.

Ensure you look at the following factors:

- **Latest Ofsted reports** – How is the school doing? Has it improved since the last inspection? What are the areas that it needs to improve on? Do these areas fit your skillset?
- **School results and performance** – How is the school performing in national league tables and against headline measures? Has this improved recently? Is there a trend of improvement over time?
- **Website** – What does the website portray about the school? Is it the type of school you'd want to work in? Are there areas that are visible from the website that you know you could improve on or have an impact on?
- **Social media** – What news stories and updates are being shared with the community? Does it feel like a school that you'd be proud to be part of?
- **Google search** – Search the school and see what it throws up. Are there any recent press articles that may give you cause for concern about the school?

Chapter 4 takeaway

Teaching tip

Take your time over choosing the right school for this crucial period in your career. If you have no need to jump ship quickly, then look at all the information you have at your disposal and make a decision that is right for you, your career and your family. Opportunities will always come up; it's just about waiting for the right one.

Pass it on

When looking at different schools, ask your colleagues what they might know about specific schools. Usually somebody knows someone who works there or you may find that someone in your school used to work there. Get their opinion on what it's like to work there, what the leadership is like and why they left. Reflect on their opinions, but remember that there are always two sides to every story.

CPD book club recommendation

Leadership Matters by Andy Buck
(See bibliography)

Bloggers' corner

'Choose the right school' by the *Times Educational Supplement* (*TES*)
(Link in bibliography)

TO DO LIST:

- ❑ Decide how far away you are prepared to travel for a new role. Work out a radius and make a list of the towns or schools that may fall into that area.
- ❑ Think about the type of school that you would like to work in.
- ❑ Start to do your research on schools that have opportunities that fall into both the previous two bullet points.
- ❑ Read *Leadership Matters* by Andy Buck.
- ❑ Read 'Choose the right school' on the TES website.

5

Preparing your application

After reading the first few chapters, you should hopefully be confident enough to begin applying for senior leadership roles. In Stage 2, let's take a look at planning your application, preparing for interviews and how to land that first senior leadership job.

Once a role has caught your eye and you have done all your research to ensure it is right for you (see previous chapters), then it's time to get down to preparing your application. This is a crucial stage in the overall process and its importance shouldn't be underestimated. Senior leadership posts usually attract between 30 and 50 applications, so what you put down on paper and how you do it will be key to gaining the opportunity to be interviewed for the post. Think to yourself, 'How will my application stand out from the crowd?'

The first stage in any process in preparing your application is to download or request the job specification and person specification. It is essential that you take the time to read and fully understand the information in these documents so that you can truly understand what type of person the school are looking for. A common mistake that people make is not fully understanding what the school want and, instead, they just talk about how good they are and what they can bring to the school, which might be very different to what the school have asked for.

Finally, before you put pen to paper, it is important to know what skills and experience will be tested via the application process and which skills will be tested at interview. This should be clearly labelled via a key. The shortlisting team will use this as a checklist when reading your application. If you don't meet the criteria and evidence the skills that they are looking for at this stage of the process, then you're likely to be overlooked.

Letter of application

A letter of application is required by most schools for the positions that they advertise. This should not be mistaken for an email that merely has the application form attached to it. An unstructured letter is the first task to see whether you are literate and can write a professional letter home to parents, or write a report for any stakeholder audience. A good letter should sell yourself and tell the story of who you are and why you want to work at that school. It should also demonstrate your passion and commitment to education, including why you are specifically applying for the role at that school, and it shouldn't just look like a standard letter written for a number of jobs. This is very important and it might just be the edge that you need to get a chance to showcase yourself at interview. Add some of the research you have already done on the school (see Chapter 4) into the letter (school vision, key areas for improvement from recent Ofsted reports or examination results, etc.) so it shows you have taken the time to be interested in the school you are applying for. As a senior leader who has shortlisted applications for positions over a number of years, what I'm looking for is someone who clearly wants to work at *our* school, not someone who has used the same letter for a number of jobs, hoping to land one of them.

The trick to convincing the shortlisting team that you are a person worthy of consideration for interview is making them imagine you in the role. Talk about what the school are looking for and how you would be successful at that based on your previous experience and current skills. Remember that the school will have in mind the role that they want you to do, so putting yourself in those shoes, metaphorically, will help the team start to visualise you in that role. The only thing to bear in mind is that your letter shouldn't be a novel. Keep it down to a maximum of two sides of A4, unless otherwise specified. Any more than two sides usually turns people off and demonstrates a lack of ability to be concise.

In getting to this stage of your career you have probably had previous experience of writing a couple of (if not more) letters of application. It is very interesting and worthwhile to locate these letters to see how far you have come since you wrote them. This will not only give you confidence from seeing everything you have achieved since that point, but there may also be some sections of the letter that you really like and that you would like to use again. However, if you have got to this position without the experience of having to write a letter for a position of responsibility, or you feel that you still need some significant help and development on how to structure your letter, a great place to start is Paul Ainsworth's book *Middle Leadership* from the Bloomsbury CPD Library. Paul breaks down the essential components of a letter of application paragraph by paragraph.

Application form

Application forms tend to be fairly standard items nowadays, but it is important not to treat this as just a formality. Even though most application forms look similar and they are all broken down into sections with specific questions to answer (unlike a letter of application that is completely without any guidance or framework), it is surprising how many people fall down at this stage due to a lack of quality.

Although this sounds obvious, it is essential to answer every question on the form and not miss anything out. If it's on the form, then it's important. Take time to read the question and understand what it is asking you for before you begin. We hear ourselves saying this to our students, but it's just as important to do it ourselves, especially when you only have a few bits of paper to showcase your suitability for interview.

I expect that every school these days will send you a digital copy of the application form to fill out. Make sure you word process your application and do not handwrite it. An application looks far more professional if it is typed, it is easier to read and it will help you to get more information into each section.

Aside from checking if you meet the criteria and person specification, senior leadership teams who have been trained on safer recruitment (every school is required to have at least one person on a shortlisting and interview panel trained in safer recruitment) are looking for gaps in employment. Gaps in employment might be legitimate for a variety of reasons, but it is important that you explain these in your application. Failure to do that casts doubt over why you have not been in employment and then raises questions about whether you might be hiding something.

References

References are an essential part of the application process and it is vital that you understand what a school is looking for. At this level it is imperative that one of your references is your current headteacher. Just like having gaps in your employment history, an application from a middle leader that doesn't include their headteacher as a reference will certainly raise questions. If you are at a stage where you feel for one reason or another that you can't include your headteacher as a reference, then you need to think very carefully about who you do choose. Secondly, your additional reference should be someone who knows you well professionally. Normally this will be another senior leader or a line manager who knows the impact you have made. Try to stay clear of people you haven't worked with for a few years. The reference should back up your abilities, experience and professionalism to date, not at a point in history.

Basic mistakes

Once you have completed your application, it is vital to go back over it with the job specification and person specification to hand. Tick off all the areas that they are testing at the application stage and make sure you have covered them all. Missing out key information at this stage can see you thrown out of the race.

Once you are confident that you have included all the desired information, get someone else to proofread your letter and application form. Trying to proofread your own work is virtually impossible because your eyes skip over the small typos and mistakes and focus on the key messages that you are trying to communicate. It is surprising how many letters and application forms that I have read contain errors and mistakes. If you can't write a letter without multiple basic errors, especially in this day and age of spellcheckers and word processing tools, then the chance of you being given the opportunity to lead a school is going to be pretty slim.

Take any opportunities on offer

Most schools will offer you the chance to either visit the school or speak to the headteacher prior to submitting your application. My advice would be to take every opportunity that is available to you as this shows your enthusiasm and keenness for the job.

Visit the school

Your current headteacher must be sympathetic to letting you visit the school, so don't feel that you can't ask.

There are two reasons for visiting:

1. To learn more about the school to see if it is the right school for you (see Chapter 4).
2. To show your enthusiasm and to try to create a good first impression that will help put a face to a name for the headteacher and shortlisting team.

Most schools will designate a few slots when you can visit the school. Some will be in the school day and some will be after so that they cater for everyone's availability. In my experience I would strongly suggest visiting in school time so that you can truly experience what it is like. A building with no children in can be soulless and it can be difficult to gain a true picture of what the school is like.

When you visit the school, go round with your eyes truly wide open. Look at the standard of uniform, litter, wall displays and everything that can build up a picture of the school. Think about the staff whom you meet or bump into during your tour. What impression do they give you of the school and what it is like to work there? Go with a list of questions in your head that you might want answering.

Lastly, it is a perfect opportunity to gauge exactly how far away the school is. This becomes even better if your visit is around the bookends of the day so you can drive to the school in rush hour, gaining a more authentic feel for how long it would take you every day.

Telephone call with the headteacher

In some cases there is an offer of a phone call with the headteacher of the school you are applying to. This can be either as an addition to or as an alternative to a visit. Taking up this opportunity lets you ask any specific questions you have that you maybe feel you either can't or haven't been able to ask on the tour. You may also get the opportunity to sell yourself during the call and add more of a personal touch to your application. However, be aware that the main purpose of the call is for you to ask the headteacher some questions about the school, its direction and anything else you may want to know. It should not be treated as an opportunity to just talk about yourself unless you are specifically asked a question about your experience or suitability for the role. The skill is to try to weave into the discussion some of your suitability and passion for the role when the opportunity presents itself, rather than making it the focus of your call.

Timing your application right

Although you will be given a clear deadline of when your application is required to be submitted by, it is worth thinking about when you might want to submit it. Submitting your application just before the deadline means that it just gets added to the box of applications with everyone else. Although you don't want to rush your application, you might want to consider the possible benefits of submitting your application early. An early application can sometimes be read as soon as it arrives, thus giving you the opportunity to create a good impression in isolation from everybody else. You just might stick in someone's mind as a candidate that they really want to see at interview.

Digital footprint

The final aspect to be aware of in the application process, which certainly wouldn't have been a factor 20 years ago, is what your digital footprint says about you. Lots of senior leaders (including me) will probably Google you or search for you on social media sites such as Twitter, Facebook, etc. What your digital footprint says about you can be quite eye-opening. Even a private social media account can be viewed if the person searching happens to be friends with someone you know. As a rule of thumb, never post anything you would be unhappy with your employer seeing. Try doing a Google search of yourself now. What impression would you get of yourself if you were an employer? What does your biography or profile say about you? And what type of comments are you posting on open social networks such as Twitter? Would any of these cause concern to a potential employer?

Chapter 5 takeaway

Teaching tip

Remember that unless you know the shortlisting panel, or have worked at the school previously, your application is the only information that the school will know about you. Take your time to make sure this is as good as it can possibly be. When a shortlisting team are faced with reading between 30 and 50 applications, yours needs to stand out from the rest. Any basic errors could immediately mean it lands on the 'no' pile.

Pass it on

If you still feel you need some guidance from someone, ask your colleagues at school. Think about people who may have recently been through an application process for a senior leadership position and ask for their advice and guidance. They may be willing to share their letter of application with you, or be your professional proofreader.

CPD book club recommendation

Bloomsbury CPD Library: Middle Leadership by Paul K. Ainsworth
(See bibliography)

Bloggers' corner

'Preparing and applying for your first headship' by Stephen Tierney
Twitter handle: @LeadingLearner
(Link in bibliography)

TO DO LIST:

- ☐ Construct your letter of application and complete your application form.
- ☐ Decide on your two references and ask them personally if they are willing to be your reference.
- ☐ Check over your application to ensure you have covered all of the essential criteria.
- ☐ Get someone to proofread your application for basic mistakes.
- ☐ Take up any opportunity to visit the school (preferably in school time).

❏ Think about when you want to submit your application.
❏ Check out what your digital footprint says about you.
❏ Refer to Paul Ainsworth's *Middle Leadership* book for tips on writing your covering letter.
❏ Read 'Preparing and applying for your first headship' by Stephen Tierney.

6 Preparing for interview

Getting to this stage hopefully means you have carefully chosen the right job opportunity for you, done your research on the school and prepared a great application that has landed you an interview. Getting this far is an achievement in itself, but this is where the competition really hots up. In my experience of having been through two separate senior leadership interviews and also having been the senior lead for interview panels that designed many other senior leadership interview days, I can say that it's generally a game of 'survival of the fittest'! Any thoughts you've got of turning up to just teach a lesson followed by a formal interview may as well be forgotten. This will probably be your biggest professional challenge to date and one that will really test how well you can perform under pressure. Most interviews for senior leadership posts now run over a two-day schedule, usually comprising six candidates, with a potential cut after day one. The two-day schedule will be packed with tasks, tests and opportunities to find out everything about you as a professional.

Although you will have been through a teaching interview previously, many of you might have been in the same school for the majority of your career and only had internal promotion interviews. Going on an external interview can be very different and if you haven't done it for a while, it can be a tough experience.

Whatever your experience of external interview situations, as mentioned in Chapter 4, it is unacceptable to not have done your homework on the school. With the amount of information publicly available on the internet, together with the information that the school sent you about what they are looking for, being underprepared is simply not an option. Remember that although the school want to find out about how good you are, they are also looking to see what you know about the school, how passionate you are about working with them and whether you are the right person for that specific role. Being able to demonstrate that you have taken the time to know everything you can about the school will go a long way in demonstrating your desire to be part of their team and not anyone else's.

Interview day tasks and activities

Although every senior leadership interview will be slightly different, most will follow a format that may include several of the following tasks and activities.

Teach a lesson

Even though the role that the school are looking for is a position of leadership, any school worth their salt will probably still want to assess how good you are as a teacher. Being able to lead by example is one thing that inspires confidence in everyone around you. However, due to the very nature of the fact that there is a good chance that everyone on interview could be specialists in different subjects, this makes the logistics of the day almost impossible. What a lot of schools are tending to do now is level the playing field and get all the candidates to teach a PSHE-style lesson. This does two things. Firstly, it takes you out of your comfort zone, something you'll have to do regularly as a senior leader. Having the ability to transfer your skillset as a classroom teacher over into another subject when required is great to see. Secondly, it allows the school to benchmark you all against the same criteria. They can set you all the same topic to teach and can see how you all go about this in different ways. Be prepared for this and don't be alarmed if you're asked to teach out of your normal subject specialism. The task is designed to be hard and to see who can adapt their skillset into a different context.

Observe a lesson

If the role you are applying for has a teaching and learning responsibility, it may be that you are asked to observe a lesson on interview. Clearly, if you are going to be observing staff in your new role and holding people to account for their classroom performance, you will need to demonstrate a sharp and accurate eye for knowing what quality looks like. This might be in the form of a live lesson observation at the back of a class, or more likely it will be a recorded lesson that you will all sit and watch together before making your judgements on the strengths and areas for development. It is also, then, quite likely that you will be asked to feed back to either that member of staff or a stand-in from the interview panel, to coach them through the next steps in their development.

In-tray exercise

You will normally be given a list of approximately ten items that have landed on your desk and you need to prioritise them in order of how and when you will deal with them. Look out for any safeguarding issues that clearly need to be dealt with immediately. The other thing to note is that some schools will give you way more issues than you can physically deal with on your own. This is done on purpose to see if you can use your delegation skills as a leader and get the people in your teams or the people that you line manage to take on some of these issues. Don't be afraid to mention this within this task.

Data task

With so much data to judge performance against, a school could pick any number of data sources for you to analyse. The most common type of data task that schools now use is an extract from a school performance analysis tool. However, due to the vast range of data available in these documents, it could be from any number of headline measures. Typically, you will be given a specific amount of time to make sense of the data, followed by writing up a brief development plan or planning a presentation on what you would do next as a senior leader in charge of this area. This could be anything from closing the gap in attendance and punctuality of various subgroups, to the performance of white British pupil premium boys in EBacc subjects. Remember though – this task can be practised beforehand as part of your preparation for interview. Use your research on the school to try to prioritise what you highlight in the time you have. Some schools will give you more information than you can handle to see if you can pick out the key priorities.

Presentation

Aside from the possible presentation related to the data task, you may also be given a specific topic to present on. This will usually be related to the post you are applying for. For example, it might be centred around curriculum change, behaviour management or safeguarding (an opportunity to again demonstrate your knowledge of the school and its key priorities). These are normally delivered to the interview panel, but I have organised a presentation task for a teaching and learning post where I got all the candidates to deliver a 30-minute professional development session to a group of staff and governors. Clearly the number of topics that you could be handed are endless; however, the way you present with confidence and clarity is just as important as the content that you present. Being a leader, you need to be able to stand up in front of a group of staff and make them believe in you. The panel will be specifically looking at whether you have the energy, enthusiasm and character to inspire their staff.

Group task

Working as part of a team is just as important in a senior leadership position as it is anywhere else in your career path. Organisations in any field don't want to employ a staff full of alpha males who will constantly battle against each other to have their ideas heard. Great teams work with one another, understanding each other's individual characteristics so they can get the very best out of their time together. In a group task situation, all the candidates will be brought into a room together and then given a problem to work through, requiring a clear plan of action at the end. The interview panel will observe all interactions between the candidates and how they work well together, especially when there are disagreements over strategies and solutions. The key here is not to be too dominant; show that you can take on board other people's suggestions and ideas, but don't be too quiet either. In all my experience of interviews, this is the task that I have found to be the hardest to get the balance right as a candidate on the day.

Student panel

The views of the students in any interview process are very important and shouldn't be underestimated. These are the people you are serving and they have a very sharp eye for quality. They can usually spot a fake at 100 metres! The panel is usually made up of the school council, with a range of year groups represented. Although the panel might have had some of their questions written for them, what they want to know is 'How will the school be better for the students under your leadership?' They'll be looking to see if you are here for them, or just for yourself. Treat the students with the utmost respect and be careful not to patronise them. They will know their stuff and won't want to be talked down to. Treat them like you would a panel of staff or governors.

Staff panels

To find out how broad your understanding and experience of whole-school leadership goes, it is quite often the case that panel interviews will be chaired by different members of the senior leadership team or middle leaders on specific topics. Think about all the Ofsted areas that we talked about in Chapter 2. Panels may be set up for teaching and learning, student outcomes and personal development, behaviour and welfare. These panels will test your knowledge on a wide variety of areas so that even if you are only going to be leading on one of those areas, you can demonstrate a broad and balanced view of school leadership. Realistically, you can't be the very best leader in one isolated area without having a good knowledge of all the other areas. Showing that you can link these areas together will do you no harm whatsoever. Remember – everything you do on interview, from entering the building to eating your lunch, will probably be commented upon. All eyes will be on you and will be reporting back.

Formal interview

If you've managed to survive the previous set of gruelling tasks, you'll now be in line for the formal interview. At this stage, there may only be two or three of you left in the process. It is fairly commonplace for a number of governors to be part of the formal interview panel, even if they haven't been part of a panel within the schedule previously. Remember that this is your final chance to impress the panel. Most of your knowledge has probably already been tested throughout the day (or two days), so now it's about you filling the panel with confidence that you can lead this school. What people sometimes forget at interview is that the headteacher and the panel are looking for a person that they can work with, not just a walking data machine or Ofsted framework. They need to see the real you. A smile and a touch of humour in the right place can go a long way to letting them get to know the real you behind the guard of a formal interview.

Personal preparation

One of the biggest mistakes to make in preparing for the two-day interview process is to concentrate too much on what the day might look like and what you need to do, whilst forgetting about yourself. Like I said right at the start of this chapter, a senior leadership interview is the survival of the fittest. You need to be the very best you that you can be, and that means being mentally and physically ready. Here are some quick tips to ensure you are at your very best.

- **Rest and sleep** – In the run-up to your interview date, get some quality rest and sleep. Your mind will be tested to the limit with multiple tasks and activities one after the other on the day, so make sure you have given your body every opportunity to be in peak condition.
- **Clear the decks** – If you make it through day one, you'll no doubt be given a task to prepare for overnight (see presentation task). You will want to give this your full attention, whilst still getting a good night's sleep. Make sure that you clear some space in your diary to do this.
- **Pick your clothes** – The last thing you want on the morning of an interview is to be stressing about what you are going to wear. Get this worked out in your mind as soon as possible. Go for something that is smart, but will make an impression. Think carefully about the message you want to convey with your outfit. Do you want to wear bright colours to show your outgoing and confident side, or do you go for something more toned down to reflect a more businesslike approach?
- **Snacks and drinks** – Taking a personal supply of snacks and drinks in your bag can be just the home comfort that you need in between those mentally and physically demanding tasks. Imagine going back to your staffroom base for a five- or ten-minute break between activities and being able to reach into your bag to grab a bar of your favourite chocolate and a can of pop. This just might be the 'pick me up' that you need to be firing on all cylinders again!
- **The route** – By now you should have already visited the school or driven the route, so this shouldn't be too much of a worry. However, if you haven't already done so, you need to work out the route you are going to take and roughly how long it will take you. Feeling pressured to get there on time in your car on the morning of an interview can send you into a tailspin before you even start. Getting there late can be the worst of bad impressions to set.

Chapter 6 takeaway

Teaching tip

Remember that the only thing you are looking to do at interview is be the very best version of you that you can be. Don't get caught up worrying about anybody else on the day in terms of who they are or what they can do. Lots of people will talk a good game and try to intimidate you, making you feel that they are the favourite for the job. Take what they say with a pinch of salt and try to shut off when they are talking shop about all of their 'achievements'. Find a quiet space in the staff room or your interview base and just focus on you and how amazing you are. Don't get caught up in trying to compete against other people. Let other people waste their energy on that.

Pass it on

Ask your colleagues to talk you through some of their experiences on interview day. You might be able to pick up some other valuable tips from them. Through your networking, you may also be able to find out the type of tasks that the specific school you have applied to use on interview day. Finding someone who has been on interview there previously, or who knows someone who has worked there, might give you a valuable 'heads up' on what is to come.

CPD book club recommendation

The Leader's Guide to Presenting by Tom Bird and Jeremy Cassell
(See bibliography)

Bloggers' corner

'Securing that leadership position' by Jon Tait
Twitter handle: @TeamTait
(Link in bibliography)

TO DO LIST:

- [ ] Do your homework on the school, its current performance and areas for development based on its latest Ofsted report.
- [ ] Prepare yourself mentally and physically for the biggest test of your educational career.
- [ ] Know how to get to the school, the route you'll take and how long it will take you.
- [ ] Read *The Leader's Guide to Presenting* by Tom Bird and Jeremy Cassell.
- [ ] Read my blog post 'Securing that leadership position'.

7

Visiting your new school

Getting to this stage should mean that you've been successful in securing your first senior leadership post. Congratulations! In the following chapters, we'll take a look at how you can hit the ground running in your new job, from day one.

Now you've landed your first senior leadership position, you'll no doubt be extremely excited to get started. However, you must remember that you still have an important role to play at your existing school. It is easy to start switching your mental focus to your new role, and the excitement of a new challenge can suddenly take priority over some of the less exciting things you may have to do in your current school. However, you have a duty of care to the students to be your best until the end and ensure that what you leave in terms of handover allows them to experience minimal impact. It is also worth noting that finishing your current job on top form can also be just as important as starting your new one with a bang. How you operate and handle your business in your last few weeks will create a lasting impression of you at the school. People will remember their last interactions with you and these are what you may be remembered by. The other thing to remember is that you never know where your career will take you, whether you'll be back at the school in some capacity or whether you'll end up working with your colleagues or line managers again at some stage. Showing that you are still committed to the school right up until your last day will go a long way to making people remember you as a true professional.

During the transition time between getting your job and then starting, it's also worth thinking about how you'll tackle the big issues facing you in your new role. Having been through the interview process and read what the role entails, you should already have in your mind the areas you'll be responsible for and how they fit into the school development plan based on the previous Ofsted report or set of results. Taking the time to formulate your vision for the role, read around the subject and plan out how you'll move the school forward in this area is really important. Your new team will want to know what your vision for school improvement is right away. Being able to hit the ground running when you start, build staff confidence in you and make an impact as quickly as you can should be your main priorities.

Alongside still doing your current role to the best of your ability, you'll also probably want to visit your new school to enable a smooth transition into the role. The last thing anyone wants (both the employee and the employer) is a first day where you are like a fish out of water. Making one or more visits to the school prior to your role commencing can significantly reduce this feeling on both sides. Most schools will release you for a day to help facilitate this. Headteachers know that they'd ask another school to release one of their staff for a day if newly appointed to their school, so need to expect to return the same favour to someone else. Usually this will be negotiated between the two headteachers to find a suitable date that works for both schools, but you may be involved in having to help make this happen by asking your current team to cover some of your duties for you.

Who and what to visit?

You will probably only be granted one day in school time to visit your new school, so you need to plan your visit well to ensure you get the most out of it. The other thing to do is to look at opportunities outside of your normal working hours so you can maximise your transition time.

Depending on your role and context, you might want to think about visiting one or more of the following people or events.

Headteacher

On the day of your interview you will have spoken to the headteacher, but will probably not have been able to have a strategic conversation about your role; you will have been mixed up in the excitement of getting the job, together with the stress of the day. Whatever was said to you on the day in terms of your new role will probably not have gone in. It is therefore good to set up a meeting with the headteacher where you can sit down together and talk through the role and the specific direction that they would like you to go in. This chat will be pivotal to you finding out the headteacher's vision for the school and any other background or contextual information that will impact upon it.

Current post holder

Making time to visit the current post holder can sometimes be overlooked, but is essential in any effective handover. Meeting this person will let them talk you through what they have done (and maybe where they were going to next if they had stayed). Ask them to talk you through how far they got with the development plan and how successful they have been in reaching school targets. They should be able to tell you what to look out for and any barriers in place and will give you a run down on your team and their individual strengths and development points. This information can be golden and should save you hours and hours when you first start, but shouldn't be exclusively used to make predetermined judgements on staff. Be wary if you feel the member of staff has an axe to grind with anybody on leaving. Try to triangulate the information they give you with the headteacher so you know you can rely on it being accurate.

SLT meeting

Attending as many SLT meetings as you can between the time you get the job and when you start your role can be very important in your transition. Not only will it let you become more familiar to your new team and enable you to get to know them, but it will also let you get up to speed very quickly on the big issues that the school are facing. Most SLT meetings will be scheduled after school, so that should make them fairly accessible for you depending on how far away you live or work from your new school. Although you will feel part of this team going forward, it's always right to ask permission from the headteacher for you to attend these meetings.

Your team

Having the opportunity to sit down with the team you will be leading, prior to your arrival, is seriously worth considering. This is a great opportunity to start communicating some of your vision for the area of the school you are responsible for, whilst letting the team really get to know you. They are bound to have questions about your vision, direction and even your experience to date. These questions are not the type of things they'd ask you in front of the whole SLT, but in a smaller, more informal team meeting they'll feel more comfortable. This is also a great opportunity to ask them the same type of questions that you might have asked the current post holder. Identifying what has stopped the team being successful previously (if that is the case), and any barriers that they believe are in their way, is just the information that you need. Armed with this information you can really set your mind to making some quick wins and demonstrating your impact immediately.

Significant events on the school calendar

A good thing to do once you get the job is to ask the headteacher or someone from the HR or admin team to get you a copy of the school calendar. Attending some of the more high-profile events in the calendar before you even start the job shows a real sense of commitment and passion for the job. Events like school concerts, rewards evenings and even parents' evenings all require a significant amount of SLT support to run smoothly. If you have the time and you can offer your support to the evening, you begin to show your team that you are more than prepared to help out on the ground whenever needed. By being at these events, you might also be able to pick up some valuable information about the standards and procedures that the school use. Looking at them with a fresh pair of eyes and not being too close to the events from an organisational point of view lets you be critical or complimentary without any personal prejudice. This feedback to the headteacher or organising teams can be some of the best and most accurate feedback they get. Just be careful that you don't go in all guns blazing and start tearing the school down before you even start!

What to find out?

With your visits being limited, it's vital to have a plan of what you want to find out and make sure you are focused on achieving that. Depending on your role and the specific tasks you have been charged with, your focus for finding out information will be slightly different in every case. However, here are some generic areas that you might find useful in getting to know.

School development plan and targets

It is highly unlikely that the whole-school development plan will have been shared with you during your interview, so it will be certainly worth trying to get your hands on it. This will enable you to see the bigger picture of where the school is going and demonstrate where your role and your team fit into this vision. This will be a key document to use when planning your own strategy of school improvement because you will be able to see what has been achieved already and what has been planned to happen next. The last thing you want to do is either reinvent the wheel or divert away from the school development plan too much unless directed by the headteacher.

Day-to-day procedures and policies

Most schools have a staff handbook that outlines the general day-to-day procedures and policies for staff. Taking a look through this will give you a good flavour of the current policies on things such as behaviour management, teaching and learning, assessment and feedback, etc. Not only will this give you an idea of the leadership of each area and the strategies used for consistency and to raise outcomes, but it will also give you a head start for when you begin teaching in the school. Some schools now have this available online so you can access it at home at your leisure. Speak to one of the admin or HR staff and they should be able to grant you access to it.

Email access

Getting access to email communication as soon as you can might be one of the best things you can do. Asking to be added to the SLT email group and being copied into the SLT communication threads can help keep you in the loop of what's going on even before you start. This will help you pick up things a bit easier at the SLT meetings that you visit (see earlier in this chapter) because you have been in the loop throughout the week on certain issues. Getting access also allows you to get in contact with your team, share ideas and ask any questions rather than having to wait until either your designated visit days or when you start your role.

Your teaching timetable

In most cases you will also still be required to teach for a certain part of the week as well as being a senior leader. This will obviously be on a reduced timetable, but you will still be held accountable for the results in your classroom. As a senior leader, demonstrating that you can walk the walk as well as talk the talk is extremely important. Finding out what you are teaching and when you are teaching it is therefore essential. Like I mentioned in Chapter 6 about being able to teach outside of your comfort zone, you may find that you are teaching another subject. This can be very daunting, but getting to know your new routine as soon as you possibly can will help you prepare for this extra challenge.

Schemes of learning

If you do find yourself teaching (like most of you will do), it is always useful to check with the head of department to find out which examination board they are following and the scheme of work that they are using. As you will know if you've been a head of department previously, examination boards can differ significantly from each other in terms of the requirements for subject content and assessment. You may also be starting a job mid-year, so finding out where a class is up to, what their progress has been and what their targets are is going to be vital.

Your office

Getting to know where your office will be and what it will look like will let you start to plan how you'll make yourself at home. Little things such as photographs for your desk or posters for your wall can then be thought about, so that when you start, it already feels like home. This will be really important in the first few weeks in the job. Everything will feel different if you are in a new school, but if you are going back to your office with a few home comforts, it makes a big difference.

Holiday opening times

In the vast majority of cases, you will be starting your new role after a period of school holiday. Finding out when the school will be open during that time is well worth knowing. The ability to come in throughout the holiday to set up your desk, kit out your office and even just bring in some files or books will make you feel so much more prepared than having to do it on your first day.

Chapter 7 takeaway

Teaching tip

Once you have been successful in landing your first senior leadership post, try to get your visits organised as soon as you can. Focus on what you want to know and then organise your visit and the people you need to meet accordingly. This will give you the information you need, along with putting some names to faces and building relationships that will make the transition into your new role so much easier.

Pass it on

If you're not sure what information you might need, why not ask some of your current colleagues what they would have liked to know before they started? You might find a couple of golden nuggets that everyone would have wanted to know that would have made their lives so much easier in the first days of their jobs.

CPD book club recommendation

Educating Drew by Drew Povey
(See bibliography)

Bloggers' corner

'How to build a winning team' by Jeremy Sutcliffe
Twitter handle: @Jeremysutcliffe
(Link in bibliography)

TO DO LIST:

- ❏ Speak to either the headteacher or the HR team to organise at least one visit to the school before you start.
- ❏ Get the two schools to negotiate the most suitable date for a visit.
- ❏ Plan out what you'd like to know and who you'd like to meet.
- ❏ Look at the school calendar to see if there are any significant events coming up that you'd like to attend.
- ❏ Get access to email and be added to the senior leadership mailing group.
- ❏ Read *Educating Drew* by Drew Povey.
- ❏ Read 'How to build a winning team' by Jeremy Sutcliffe.

8 Understanding the school

The next stage in preparation for your new role is to obtain all the information that you will need to enable you to be as successful as you can, as quickly as you possibly can. Although this isn't going to be a task that you can ever feel is completed (due to the fast-changing dynamic context that we are all in), there are lots of pieces of information that you will need when you begin a new role like this. Going into a new role blind, without the essential background information that we'll discuss here, can either set you off in the wrong direction or place significant barriers in your way. It is essential for a leader to be well-informed and have all the knowledge and information at their fingertips so that they can plan their strategies for school improvement. Without this knowledge, poor decisions can be made that lead to schools stagnating or, in some cases, going backwards.

Although the information and knowledge that you'll require in every one of the following areas will be vastly different, and in some cases more significant than in other schools, it is important to get a broad picture of your new school.

School history

Finding out the significant history of your new school is respectful to both the school and its community, together with being interesting to you. You might find out about the journey the school has been on, significant developments along the way and maybe even some notable ex-students that have gone on to be in the public eye. Taking the time to know and understand the history of the school really shows that you care about it and that you are investing yourself in the school community. It is natural for staff to be testing out your character and motives in the first few months of your job, so being able to demonstrate a complete commitment and 'buy in' to the school will go a long way to winning people over.

School context

Understanding the context that the school is in is vital. You will have started to do this as part of your interview preparation, but there will now be more extensive opportunities to find out much more detailed knowledge, now that you've got the job. Without an in-depth knowledge of the following areas, you can't lead your school effectively, so you need to make it your priority to not only have this information, but truly understand it.

- **School performance** – Headline performance measures over the past three to five years. Is the school on an upward trajectory? How is the school performing in general? Is this an opportunity to build on and celebrate, or is it a concern?

- **Ofsted** – How did the school perform in its latest Ofsted inspection? Was this an improvement on the inspection before? What are the strengths and areas for development that have been identified by Ofsted? Has this changed since the last inspection? Is the school due an inspection soon?
- **Direction** – Where is the school going? What direction does the headteacher see the school moving in? Is the priority focus to move up to the next Ofsted rating? Is the school looking to be part of a MAT? Is the school pursuing any other areas of specialism or designation?
- **Local authority context** – How is the school performing in relation to the other schools in the town or the local authority? How is the local authority performing nationally? Is there any pressure on the local authority to raise standards?
- **League tables** – Where does the school sit in the most recently published local and national performance tables? How does this compare to the last three to five years? Has there been an improvement? Does the position of the school in these performance tables bring any pressure to the school?
- **Values and vision** – What are the current school values and vision of the headteacher? It's okay to have your own vision and values, but you may find that you are working with someone else's in the first instance and need to make them your own for a period of time.

Data

Although you will no doubt have been given some data to look over at interview, and you will have tried to get your hands on anything you could find about the school performance ahead of this date, there are still lots of pieces of data that you will need to know in order to be as successful and effective as you can.

- **Headline measures** – How does the school stack up against all of the headline measures? Where are the strengths and where are the areas that require improving? How will your new role help to improve on these areas? How does this fit into your strategic plan for school improvement?
- **Analyse School Performance** – If you haven't already managed to get your hands on a copy of the school's most recent performance data, then you need to make this your priority. All of the headline measures can be found in there, along with a whole host of other contextual information about the school, its make-up and its performance across a range of measures.
- **Trends** – Although you may be able to get your hands on the most recent data set, you need to compare this with the data for the previous two to three years. Is there a trend of improvement or decline? Are there any spikes or anomalies? If there are any trends and patterns emerging, what impact will this have

on your next Ofsted inspection? How does this need to be reflected in your strategies and development plans?

- **In-school data** – Whilst your external examination data is the data that is publicly available and included in performance tables, your in-school data for your current learners is also extremely important. Knowing where your current cohorts are and what they are predicted to get will also be a significant factor in your development planning. For example, what are you going to do about the fact that your current Year 10 cohort are extremely weak in maths? This is now an increasingly important set of data that is analysed by Ofsted to show the potential journey that the school is on and whether the school has the capacity to improve.
- **Targets and predictions** – All of the above sets of data and information should then be feeding into your targets and predictions. These are key pieces of data to know and have at your fingertips so that you know what you are aiming to achieve.

Local competition

Developing an understanding of who your local competition is can be very important. In this day and age of academies and parents having more choice in terms of where they send their children, education has become a business. In some contexts, getting bums on seats in Year 7 can be the biggest challenge that a school faces. Without these students, schools can be faced with making staffing reductions, which can change the whole direction of a school. It is therefore good to know what the local picture looks and feels like in terms of where people send their children and why, together with how your school USP will attract families.

- **Who?** Who are the schools that you are competing with for students every year?
- **Where?** Where are these schools? Are they on your doorstep, meaning they will always be competition? Or are they in a different area of the town, but are recruiting students in what you would have historically considered your catchment area?
- **Why?** Why are these schools in competition for the same students as you? Has this always been the case? Or have certain schools started to recruit students from certain schools that you would historically have had big cohorts from? Is the recent performance of your school having any impact on this?

Student population forecasts

Together with understanding your local competition, it is also worth thinking about the general student population forecasts over the coming years. The birth rate in the local area and the number of students currently attending the local primary schools will have a significant impact on your school population. If you are in a position where you have strong competition for places, together with a falling birth rate in the town, you can be sure that you are going to be in for a tough and concerning time over the next few years. As a middle leader you may not have had to think about this previously, but as a senior leader you need to be fully aware that the number of students who are on roll every year will shape the school budget. Knowing that there will be a rise or a spike in student numbers, or alternatively a drop in your new intake, will enable you to plan accordingly and not be caught out when it happens. Outstanding leadership teams will have their eye on this and know what is likely to happen in the next five to ten years so that they can secure the long-term future of the school by sensible and informed financial planning.

Financial position

Your financial position as a school will be one of the biggest driving forces in being able to deliver your vision for school improvement. With cuts to school budgets and what seems to be an ever-tightening belt on school finances, it is essential that you know the position that your school is in. As a leader, you would be seen as naïve and inexperienced if you created a plan for school improvement that asked for the earth if you were in an extremely tight financial position as a school. Although your job is to have a vision, be enthusiastic and push the boundaries for what is possible, this also needs to be realistic with the resources at your disposal. Sitting down with the headteacher or your business manager will let you see the bigger picture of the financial position of the school, thus letting you understand why certain decisions need to be made, or why the school might be heading in a certain direction.

Staffing

Your school will only be as good as the teachers who work there. You can have a great vision as a senior leader, but if you haven't got the quality of staff to execute it, then it's not going to be as effective or successful as you'd originally thought. Understanding your staff is therefore vital so you can either make your plans fit your staff, or make your staff fit your plans!

- **Staff profile** – What does the staff profile look like? Is it an ageing staff with several people near retirement? Is it a relatively young profile that lacks experience but brings fresh ideas? Is there stagnation, with lots of people doing the same roles that they have done for years? What will this mean for your strategic plans? Ask the HR rep for CVs and try to know the staff before you arrive. Pictures are great to have a look at so that you can try to call staff by name once you arrive.

- **Staff performance** – How many staff have you got who require improvement in their classroom performance? Are there any staff who require formal improvement plans? How good is the CPD offer that the school currently provides? How many expert classroom practitioners do you have who may be looking for promotion in the near future?
- **Recruitment** – Has your school been able to recruit for all the required teaching positions? Have you got any non-specialists teaching in any specific areas? Are there any areas that you have had problems appointing for? Are there any long-term supply staff in? Are any staff on short-term, fixed or temporary contracts?

Threats and opportunities

In any line of business, you should take time to think about the potential threats that are either surrounding you or are on the horizon. Some of these may come from the information we have looked at above – for example, student population forecasts or local competition. Having a keen eye on these threats is essential if you want to be successful. Sticking your head in the sand and hoping that they will go away is not the approach that an outstanding leader takes. Whatever the threat and whatever the potential harm to your school, you need to be ready to tackle it as soon as you can. In most cases, even what may initially seem to be the biggest of threats and problems can be worked around by timely and well-planned strategic thinking.

It's also important not to miss the opportunities when they present themselves. These can be such things as funding, partnerships and networks that can enable you to do so much more as a school. Sometimes these opportunities are hidden in amongst other things and can even be disguised as potential threats. As you become more experienced as a senior leader you will develop a sharper eye for these and be able to take advantage of them when they present themselves.

Chapter 8 takeaway

Teaching tip

Only when you've taken the time to fully understand the school in all its diverse context, will you truly be able to move the school forward. This can be quite overwhelming in terms of the amount of data and information that you might need to absorb, but thinking about it in distinct areas might make it feel more manageable.

Pass it on

This process of understanding the school isn't (and shouldn't be) just about reading school performance data and analysing data sheets. Lots of the information can be found by simply talking to your new colleagues. They will also be the bearers of lots of interesting information that you'll not find in a school performance document. Their views and interpretations of the data and the school context might give you a more valuable viewpoint to consider.

CPD book club recommendation

Narrowing the Attainment Gap by Daniel Sobel
(See bibliography)

Bloggers' corner

'From vision to action: establishing a vision for your school' by John Tomsett
Twitter handle: @johntomsett
(Link in bibliography)

TO DO LIST:

- ☐ Obtain the information you need.
- ☐ Take time to understand it.
- ☐ Speak to colleagues for their interpretation of the information.
- ☐ Adjust or plan your strategic school improvement plans accordingly.
- ☐ Read *Narrowing the Attainment Gap* by Daniel Sobel.
- ☐ Read 'From vision to action: establishing a vision for your school' by John Tomsett.

9

Developing your vision for school improvement

In the previous two chapters, we talked about visiting your new school to gain vital information and then understanding the context and performance of the school. These two steps are absolutely crucial before you embark on formulating your vision for school improvement. This is not necessarily about what you want to do in your new role, but more about what the school needs you to do. That is not to say that there will be a road map of school improvement laid out for you already. Far from it – otherwise the school could have probably promoted someone internally to manage the development plans. You will need to have a firm grip on what needs improving before you set about planning how you are going to improve it.

In Chapter 4 we talked about picking the right school and the types of schools that fall under certain performance categories. In my experience, outstanding schools will almost certainly give you less freedom and creativity to develop your vision, because clearly, they already have systems and strategies in place that have been effective. The last thing they will want you to do is to start ripping things up and starting again. However, schools that are in need of rapid improvement, or are beginning their journey towards sustained improvement, will probably be more open to a fresh pair of eyes coming in with new ideas. It is therefore essential that you have understood the context of your new school (as described in Chapter 7 and Chapter 8), because that will underpin how much licence you have to be creative in your own vision for school improvement.

What is the vision of the school?

If you have followed the steps in Chapter 7, you should by now have taken the opportunity to visit your new school. Within this visit, you should hopefully have had a chance to sit down with the headteacher and understand his or her vision for school improvement. It is within this conversation that you will probably get the best steer on how much licence for creativity you may or may not have. Every school will be slightly different, so taking the time to find this out is extremely important.

- **In some schools**, the headteacher and the senior leadership might already know exactly where they are going and what is required next. In this situation, you will be given the development plan and told to make it happen. Your skill in this instance will be to get the staff behind the plans and for you to make them happen as quickly and as effectively as you can.
- **In other schools**, the road map for improvement might not be as clear. The headteacher may have recruited you because the current senior leadership team do not possess the knowledge or vision for improvement in a certain area. They may have tried many strategies before, but are now looking for a fresh perspective. Your skill in this instance will be to start with a blank canvas and develop a new direction for the school to go in. Once you've done this, you then also need to make it happen.

What requires improvement?

In Chapter 8 we talked about understanding the school performance data (CAT4, ALIS, ALPS, TIMSS, PISA and GL Progress Tests for international schools) and the areas for further improvement identified in the most recent Ofsted inspection report. This information is the fine detail that lies underneath the headteacher's vision for school improvement. Cross-referencing the vision with the data will enable you to see how the vision has been generated and give you specific targets and performance indicators that you should be working to meet. It may also throw up some other areas that you feel require improving. It may be that the current senior leadership team have either missed these or they didn't feel that they had the expertise to tackle them. With your skill, experience and record of improvement, you may feel that these are areas that you can have an impact on.

Another area worth noting, when looking at what the school needs to improve on, is the agenda for improvement from the DfE. When I first started teaching, closing the gaps between various subgroups of students wasn't as much of a priority as it is now. Agendas change and there are certain areas that become topical and much more important than others from time to time. Understanding what the key areas for improvement are from the point of view of the DfE and Ofsted will let you start to look at your school performance data with a sharper eye. You will then be able to zoom in on those areas and develop a vision for school improvement that will enable the school to become successful under the current frameworks of performance that we operate within.

There are also areas of school improvement that don't show up on any school performance tables. These are the areas that parents, students and the community want to see happen. These might be areas such as the quality of customer service that your front office staff provide, or the fact that students are having to queue for too long to get their lunch, or even the complaints you are receiving from local residents due to the way the students leave the site every day. This information can be gleaned from student and parental voice forums/surveys (if there are none, consider gathering this information). These areas of school improvement should not be overlooked just because they can't be measured by a school league table. These areas can sometimes be the most important things to improve on, as they have a significant impact on the reputation of the school and therefore have a bearing on pupil numbers every year. You may also find that by solving some of these issues, there is a significant knock-on effect on other areas of school improvement. For example, students waiting too long for their lunch may start skipping lunch, deciding to play instead of giving up the majority of their time waiting to eat. This might be having a negative impact on behaviour in the afternoon, because students are hungry, restless and without the necessary energy they require to be focused in lessons. By resolving your lunchtime issues, you may just solve a whole-school behaviour problem that has been plaguing the school for years.

What is your vision?

Once you have understood both the school's vision and the areas for improvement, you can then set about planning your own vision for school improvement (if you've been given licence to). Depending on the length of time that you have between getting the job and starting, you might find that this is the best time to develop this. Everyone wants to hit the ground running in a new job and your new colleagues will be looking to you straight away to test your credentials. Having the time and ability to formulate your vision before you start will give you the opportunity to begin to make an impact as soon as you walk through the door. However, this can only happen if you have taken the time and had the opportunities to complete all the tasks set out in Chapter 7 and Chapter 8. Only then will you be in a position to accurately map out the way forward for the school in your designated area of responsibility.

Assuming you've got all the information you require from the school and have understood where the school is and where it needs to go, you can then put the meat on the bones. It is at this point that you need to think specifically about how you are going to bring about improvement in your area of responsibility. Depending on your previous experience and areas of expertise, you may find planning your road map to improvement a relatively easy task to do, but in other cases it might be quite a challenge. Taking the time to focus on this before you begin the role allows you thinking and reflection time, together with the ability to look for sources of advice and inspiration. These sources of inspiration may come from colleagues you have worked with, fellow senior leaders in your professional network, or books and blogs that you have come across. Either way, you shouldn't think that your road map has to be entirely down to your own thinking. Great leaders are inspired by other great leaders and are comfortable adapting other people's ideas to fit to their own context. Being able to look at a range of strategies that have been used in other schools, alongside your own personal creative thinking, enables you to have all the ideas and resources at your disposal to make the very best plan for moving forward. Without external sources of advice or inspiration, poor planning can sometimes happen because there has only ever been one way of thinking applied to a situation. In some cases, this is why schools can underperform and why they need an external pair of eyes to freshen things up.

Priorities

Depending on the context of your new school/role, your vision for school improvement may need to be for one, three or five years. It is therefore extremely important to prioritise certain strategies. Prioritising your improvement strategies has to be done with reference to the school performance data and school inspection areas for improvement that we have talked about in Chapter 8. It is easy to focus on the areas that you know you'll enjoy, or the areas that you might have significant experience in, but if they are not the school's priorities right now, then it's a waste of time. Outstanding leaders can analyse school data and identify the priorities that will make the biggest difference in the shortest space of time.

Quick wins

Earlier in this chapter we talked about your new colleagues looking to you for impact the moment you walk in the door. By prioritising some areas that you can resolve quickly, you can start to demonstrate an impact immediately and therefore build staff confidence in you. For example, you may find out that there has been something that has been annoying staff for a long time and it's something that you can fix within a couple of weeks with a new approach. Looking for quick wins like this can increase the confidence and respect that staff have in you, almost overnight. Taking on big projects that won't show any impact for months and have you hidden away in your office working on them will not build any significant confidence on the ground. If you feel you are in this situation by necessity, think about other small quick wins that you can do alongside the bigger projects. Speak to staff and students and find out what bugs them and what could make the school a better place to be in. Then try to look for the things you can do relatively quickly.

Things change

Don't fall into the trap of thinking that your vision only has to be constructed once. In the dynamic and turbulent educational world that we find ourselves in, your vision has to be adaptable. One set of exam results, an Ofsted inspection or a change of government can render your plan almost obsolete and in need of you revisiting the drawing board. As a leader, you have the responsibility to keep your eyes on the ongoing incremental performance of the school, whilst also keeping up to date with what is going on locally and nationally. Being in a position to tweak and change your strategies in a timely fashion, based on an internal or external catalyst, will mean that you will be able to constantly meet the demands of your school, as well as the constant changing of requirements laid out by the DfE and Ofsted. Building in regular reflection time to monitor your progress and look at the changing needs around you will be time well spent.

Chapter 9 takeaway

Teaching tip

Developing your vision for school improvement should first be a fact-finding mission; then a creative planning exercise looking at how you are going to solve the issues you have identified; followed by prioritising in which order you are going to tackle each of the identified issues. Only then can you be sure that your vision and road map for improvement is fit for purpose.

Pass it on

Talking to the people on the ground in your new school can give you a fresh perspective on what you need to improve. The classroom teachers are the ones who see what is happening and are the ones who feel policy changes the most. Take their input seriously and look at ways in which you can resolve little issues quickly in order to make a big difference to them.

CPD book club recommendation

The School Leadership Journey by John Dunford
(See bibliography)

Bloggers' corner

'Great school leadership 2: vision' by Tom Sherrington
Twitter handle: @teacherhead
(Link in bibliography)

TO DO LIST:

- ☐ Understand the vision that the headteacher has for the school.
- ☐ Analyse school data and recent inspection reports to identify key areas for improvement.
- ☐ Cross-reference the areas for improvement with any local or national agendas.
- ☐ Prioritise your strategies for improvement.
- ☐ Look for any quick wins that will instantly build staff confidence in you.
- ☐ Read *The School Leadership Journey* by John Dunford.
- ☐ Read 'Great school leadership 2: vision' by Tom Sherrington.

10 Building professional relationships

Irrespective of how good you are, or how good you think you are, nothing is achieved in senior leadership without the support of the team around you. Understanding and appreciating this is going to be key to your success as a leader. There will be times when you need advice, guidance, help and even the odd reality check. It is therefore essential that there is a mutual trust and respect between you so that, no matter what, you know they'll go that extra mile for you. As you will no doubt know by now though, trust and respect don't just come from your job title; you have to earn them and work on them. Granted, in the first few weeks of your new role, staff will be out to impress you and get on the right side of you, but this will soon wear off if they find out that you are not a nice person to work for. Yes, they will do as you ask, but that's as far as it will go. No running through walls or going the extra mile. That only comes when you have the utmost respect for someone, because you know that they'd do the same for you. Like I've said in the book many times already, every school is different and will operate in a different context, but in almost every school you'll have to build up professional working relationships with the following groups of people.

Governors

The mistake that many inexperienced senior leaders make is not to go out of their way to forge strong and immediate relationships with significant members of the governing body. Over the course of your school improvement journey, you will need to rely on your governing body to support you through change management, so having their 100 per cent trust and confidence in you will make things significantly easier. As a newly appointed member of the leadership team, the best time to build up this trust and confidence is straight away. The governing body will still have you fresh in their minds after recently appointing you and will be keen to see you hit the ground running. Manufacturing opportunities to talk to the relevant members of the governing body about your vision and, in time, your impact will do you no harm whatsoever. Keeping them regularly in the loop about your plans and your progress will ensure that when the time comes for you to call on their support, they are on the same page as you.

In most schools, senior leadership teams will have designated school governors for different areas of the Ofsted framework so they can hold the leaders responsible to account. Good practice is to schedule termly meetings with your link governors so that they have regular progress updates and are formally kept in the loop. These governors should come with questions related to the school development plan or the last set of school performance indicators so that you can be challenged about the work you are doing to raise standards in your area of responsibility.

Even though these meetings are planned termly, I would always say to my link governors that they are free to schedule a visit or a learning walk whenever they like so that they feel that there is nothing to hide and that they are seeing the school as it is on a daily basis.

Fellow senior leaders

Getting to know your colleagues in your senior leadership team is a must. School improvement can be a tough road and there will be bumps and diversions along the way. Having the full support of your colleagues through these testing times is so important, especially if you are new to the school. Throughout your school improvement journey, you will have to lean on your colleagues for help and advice, because none of the areas of responsibility that we discussed in Chapter 2 are mutually exclusive. The crossover in these areas is always going to be significant, so understanding your senior colleagues' roles, and the barriers that they are coming up against, will enable you to work more collaboratively to bring about rapid improvement.

Secondly, and possibly more importantly, you are bound to need some emotional support from your fellow senior leadership colleagues along the way. Like I said in the previous paragraph, there will be some bumpy roads ahead and having the full and unconditional support of your colleagues can make all the difference. Seldom will you not need a hug, a cry or a general pick-me-up conversation during your time as a senior leader in today's educational landscape. Strong relationships are key for this. Getting to really know your colleagues lets you feel you can open up to them, but also be there to support them in their hour of need. This bond and togetherness is what successful teams pride themselves on.

There's no real complicated strategy to making this happen apart from just spending time with them. Taking the time to sit with them, talk to them and get to know them is so easy; it's just that when we are so busy, this social bonding seems to be not as important as some of the other things on our list. However, the time that you invest in people by talking to them about work and their own lives away from school will reap you the rewards in the long term. Social nights out with your colleagues can also bring people much closer together and let people see you as a real person away from the day-to-day stresses of the job. Just remember, though, that when alcohol is involved, things can sometimes go differently from how you may have envisaged them. Having a few drinks is fine, but remember that you are trying to build a positive impression of yourself to your new colleagues.

Teachers

Every senior leader worth their salt knows that without the support of the staff behind them, their vision and improvement plans mean nothing. You can't move a school forward on your own, so getting the staff on board with your vision and creating a feeling of confidence in you is absolutely crucial. If people believe in you and see your authenticity as a leader, they will follow you and your vision. In a big school, getting to know each and every member of staff in the way you might do your fellow senior leadership colleagues is going to be unrealistic; however, there are a few easy strategies that will quickly build up your professional relationships with staff, giving them confidence and trust in you as a new leader.

Visibility

Get out of your office as much as you can. One thing that people in any organisation don't like is leaders who hide away in their offices and don't know what it's like on the ground. No matter how busy you might think you are, spending time in the school corridors, the school playground or the dining hall at break and lunch time will raise your stock in the staffroom overnight. Sending that message to staff that 'I'm with you' can mean everything to some people. Also, the very nature of being out and about in the school allows you to talk to people and start to build up those professional relationships. Imagine the teacher who wasn't really sure of you coming in as a new leader in the school and was wary of you until she or he got to know you. By stopping to talk in the corridor with them at break time, you can instantly let them get to know you a bit better and have a normal conversation about the weather or what you both did at the weekend, letting them see you as a real person just like them.

Quick wins

The minute you step into the school, everyone is looking for impact from you, and there is no harsher critic on your performance than the gossips in the staffroom. In Chapter 9 we discussed the importance of quick wins in your development plans for school improvement and the impact they would have all around you. Never underestimate the power of a quick win in the staffroom. If you can find out some of the things that the staff have been moaning about for ages and are perceived to be some of the things that are making their jobs harder than they need to be, these should be top of your list of priorities. Resolving these things overnight will give you so much currency with the staffroom critics that you'll go from new boy/girl to the saviour in a matter of days! It might be as easy as just fixing the coffee machine. No matter how irrelevant some of these things might seem in the grand scheme of school improvement, you need to understand what is perceived to be important in the lives of the teachers and support staff. Once you understand this (and create a communication channel for picking up these gripes and frustrations) then you'll be able to keep your staff happy.

Start with the 'why'

Another thing that people in any organisation hate is having to do things without being told why. Leaders sometimes forget that the people on the ground don't always see the bigger picture because they haven't been privy to the same information or experience that you have. Therefore, some decisions and new policies can seem pointless, excessive and a general waste of time. The last thing you want as a new leader in a school is for your first new policy change or strategic implementation of an idea to go down like a lead balloon because the staff don't see the point behind it. Taking the time to explain the 'why' to staff is essential in getting everyone on board. In the vast majority of cases, once staff have been told why they are doing something and the benefits for either the students or the school, they'll happily get on board.

Sharing the 'why' also lets the staff feel valued and respected because you are taking the time to talk about why you have come up with your vision and why it's going to be so important. This naturally builds strong relationships between professionals, because even if you don't agree with somebody, you can at least see where they are coming from and why they have developed an idea. When we think that somebody has just plucked an idea out of the air, or won't take the time or give you the respect to tell you why they have developed their viewpoint, we begin to question their intentions.

Support staff

Support staff in any school are the unsung heroes and the people who make the school tick. They are usually some of the lowest paid staff, but do some of the most important day-to-day jobs. No matter what role you do as a senior leader, you will need significant help from the support staff in your school. Whether it's answering the phones in the school office and being the friendly face that parents and visitors see, or whether it's the administration work they do on the attendance data-crunching or the letters they send out for you, you wouldn't be able to do your job without them. Taking the time to stop and thank them can make all the difference if you are wanting to build strong and lasting positive relationships. One thing we can forget to do in our busy roles is stop and tell people how much we appreciate them and how much their jobs make a big difference to the success of the school. A quick chat, a card or a box of chocolates will go a long way with people. Your support staff are then far more likely to do that extra job for you or take that little bit of extra time if they feel openly valued and appreciated.

Chapter 10 takeaway

Teaching tip

No matter how good you think you are, you simply can't move a school forward on your own. Yes, you can formulate the vision and the detail, but the people on the ground, around you and above you, will be the people who will drive it forward. If you don't get people on board by building strong professional relationships, then you will lack the crucial support that you'll need in the long term to make your vision become a reality.

Pass it on

Talking to people builds relationships; communicating via email doesn't. Remember to get out and about as much as you can so that you can talk to people face to face. Take the time to talk to cleaners, office staff, teachers and governors. All of these people play a significant part in your school improvement plans, so they should all be treated with equal measures of respect. A positive interaction with one person can then snowball once they tell their colleagues about it.

CPD book club recommendation

Liminal Leadership by Stephen Tierney
(See bibliography)

Bloggers' corner

'Relationship building with teacher colleagues' by Jordan Catapano
Twitter handle: @BuffEnglish
(Link in bibliography)

TO DO LIST:

❑ Schedule a termly meeting with your link governors to keep them up to speed with your progress towards your targets.

❑ Get to know your fellow senior leadership colleagues by spending time with them both in and out of school.

❑ Build trust and confidence in yourself with the teaching staff by being visible around the school site whenever you can.

❑ Look for some quick wins that make the biggest difference to staff and that you can resolve as quickly as possible.

❑ Start any new initiative or directive by telling people the 'why'.

❑ Take time to say thank you to the support staff who help you every day.

❑ Read *Liminal Leadership* by Stephen Tierney.

❑ Read 'Relationship building with teacher colleagues' by Jordan Catapano.

11 Building community relationships

Although your initial focus as a new senior leader will be on what's happening inside your building, you should not underestimate the significance of building strong community relationships. In some cases, the school is the heart of the community and everything revolves around it. In these contexts, your role as a school leader becomes much wider and can become far more community-focused. Being a leader in these types of schools can enable you to have a diverse and far-reaching impact on the community. In other schools where this is not the case, there may be significant competition in the local community to be the preferred school, so your presence as a leader and what you stand for can be just as important, if not more so. In these contexts, it's vitally important to try to gain a foothold in the community so that you can begin to spread the word about the successes of your school. These opportunities will also let you help change the minds of people who may have had a negative impression of the school based on an old or inaccurate reputation.

Going back to a golden thread that I've been talking about in several chapters so far, it's about understanding your new school context as quickly as you possibly can. By finding out what role your school plays in the local community, and whether you need to have a more prominent role, you can then work out a strategy for building community relationships or further strengthening them. Whatever your school position in the community, there can never be any negative effects of strong community relationships and it's something that most schools would openly admit that they'd like to improve.

As a senior leader in your school, you can play a big part in how your school is viewed by the community. Every time you are seen, or you communicate with the different groups that I am about to discuss below, you are being judged. In turn, this leads to the formation of an opinion about your school. Try to think about how you can be the perfect ambassador for your school. What type of characteristics would you want to display to the community? And how can you create opportunities to do this?

The following groups of people are all significant groups that make up the wider community and all need to be thought about slightly differently when you are looking to strengthen your community relationships.

Parents

Out of all the groups who make up the community, parents are the most thought-about group when it comes to school leadership. However, if you really want to make this a strength of your school's community relationships, you'll need to think a little bit outside the box. If you think that just organising the standard parents' evenings throughout the year and sending reports home will cut the mustard, then you're very much mistaken. In this day and age of free communication and easy access to rich media content, you'll have to do a little bit more than you did ten years ago to satisfy the needs of some of your parents.

Using social media can be a great and cost-effective way to do this. By posting regular updates from the school on a daily or even hourly basis, you can communicate freely and easily with your parents without high costs or man hours. Schools that do this well can engage their parents in regular school news, events and updates in a friendly and sociable way, enabling parents to share this information on their own networks, thus significantly increasing the reach of your communication.

Communication doesn't also just have to be in a written format. Some forward-thinking and tech-savvy schools are now also filming short weekly video blogs from the headteacher about everything that has gone on in the last week, or important upcoming events. This is a great way to engage with your parents and a chance for them to feel like a senior leader is taking the time to talk to them personally, something that is hard to regularly do with the time constraints and pressures that the job brings.

A great way to build up some of these informal relationships is to be out on the school gate as much as you can on a morning or afternoon. Parents often stop to chat if they've got a concern and, even if it's subconscious, parents will always respect you for being out there on the gate and not tucked away in your office. By being visible to parents, they will feel your confidence in the community and know that if they need to speak to you, you are going to be far more approachable than someone who likes to hide behind their desk.

Lastly with parents, it's about taking any opportunity you can to talk to them. Whether it's at an event, on the school gate or on the phone, it's an essential part of your job. Unfortunately, lots of your parents may have a negative view of school due to their own experience as a child, and others will believe you may be a strict taskmaster just because of your position or title. By taking the time to stop and speak to people with a smile on your face, you can start to win people over pretty quickly as they begin to realise 'He was actually alright when I spoke to him'!

Residents

Local residents see the school in all its glory and all its shame. They are the houses that students walk past on the way to and from school and the ones that will unfortunately often remember you for all the negative reasons. By working with local residents, rather than against them, you can hopefully build strong bonds so that they too can be great ambassadors for your school.

Although in some cases you'll never win people over and they may always have a negative impression of your school and your students (due to an isolated incident that they haven't forgotten), most people are reasonable people who you can talk to. Once you take the time to talk to them, the vast majority will understand the problems you may face as a school when you let a thousand children loose into the community. The thing they don't like, though, is when they feel they aren't being listened to, or if you are just ignoring their calls for help. By creating a culture in school where you take every call from a local resident as seriously as a call from a parent, you'll soon begin to build up significant personal relationships with the local community. Once they know that you'll help them and act on your word to help make their community a nicer place to live, then you'll really start to see the difference.

The last thing you want in any local community around a school is local residents who don't have a good word to say about the students or the senior staff. This can be very damaging and can spread to places that you'd never imagine just by word of mouth. The opposite can be very powerful though. Sharing your success stories with your local residents and inviting them into the school to see what you are really all about can be a significant stride in building long-lasting positive relationships. A cup of tea or coffee can go a long way!

Businesses

Depending on the exact location of your school building in your local community, you may have more impact on local businesses than other schools. For example, if your school is close to a group of shops, takeaways or supermarkets, your student footfall in these areas might be quite significant. It is therefore worth remembering that, just like your local residents, these business owners or employees will probably see your school at its worst. Think about what impression you would have of a school if all you ever saw was children looking unruly, using bad language and not particularly caring for the local community and its residents. If you can have more presence in these areas before and after school, it will almost certainly reduce the amount of complaints you receive and will undoubtedly be appreciated by all. Just like the residents, if the business owners and employees know that you care about them and you are committed to doing something to help and support them, then their impression of you and the school will rocket.

It is also worth remembering the bigger businesses in the town that may not be in the immediate area, but may be able to help and support your school with great opportunities for your students. Getting out to speak to these businesses and organisations can reap major rewards. Firstly, you can begin to create a local network of business contacts who can potentially help and support events and opportunities at your school, and secondly, it can give you further opportunities to talk about the great work that your school is doing. You never know where this word of mouth goes and how far it travels. There's one thing for sure though: sending great messages into the community about your school and your successes and enabling them to speak to a real person will never be a waste of time.

Religious groups

One of the groups of people that is sometimes forgotten, but can have one of the biggest influences on forming the reputation of your school, is religious groups. Over the past few years I have appreciated this first hand, working in a very multicultural community. Underestimating the power and influence of these strong religious groups in the community is naïve. The work that these groups do, in particular related to the ongoing education and development of children and young adults, is huge. Having a local school who wants to work with them, not against them, can be a significant factor in getting your positive messages out to a larger audience.

Some schools now have formalised community groups where members of the different churches, temples and mosques come together in the school for regular updates and briefings. This demonstrates that the school is seriously interested in the different cultures and religious groups in the local area and places a real value on opening up communication channels with group leaders. This can be extremely beneficial because some of these cultures and religious groups are hard to reach with effective communication. But by having an open and regular communication line straight to the community leaders of the groups, your messages and success stories can be shared far and wide with the authenticity of them coming from a respected community leader.

Equally important is the opportunity for important information to be communicated back to school. You may find that in working closely with these religious groups you begin to find out more about what's going on in the community, upcoming festivals or events that may impact on the school or your students. Whatever format your community relationship is built on with the leaders of these groups, it's always good to have your ear to the ground.

Local media

Shouting from the rooftops about your school and its successes isn't always that easy. Yes, you can post stories and updates on your school website, but people have to make a conscious decision to go there to find out about you. By building up strong relationships with the local media, you can begin to exploit opportunities to get your message across on a far wider and more prominent scale.

The biggest thing to remember when it comes to the local media is that no matter who they are (newspaper, TV or radio), they are all looking for content to fill their publications and shows every single day. Although you'll need to choose wisely what you send and when, the chances are if you send enough high-quality content regularly, you'll be able to get quite a bit of it featured.

Just as we've also discussed in relation to residents and businesses, giving a reporter, researcher or producer the chance to come and meet you and put a face to a name will also pay dividends. In a half-hour meeting, you can introduce your school and everything that is good about it, talking about events that are coming up and the things you really stand for as a school. This will give the media outlet a great starting point for future articles or media slots when a news story comes up in the press. It may result in you being asked for a comment on a certain piece or whether the school would like to feature in a story about how a local school are tackling a national issue. Either way, by building up a positive relationship with the media, you are able to use them to your advantage and not the other way around.

Chapter 11 takeaway

Teaching tip
Never underestimate the power of strong and positive community relationships in forming an excellent reputation for your school. You must also remember that they must be worked on and certainly don't just happen by accident. Different groups of people require different approaches, but all of the groups that play a part in your local community will have a significant voice. The key to building successful and long-lasting positive relationships relies on face-to-face communication and getting out from behind your desk as a school leader and into the community.

Pass it on
When starting at a new school, ask somebody to take you into the community. Setting up some organised visits in the early days of your new role can be very beneficial. You can start to get a flavour for the diversity of the community you are now working in, together with letting the community see you in action and get to know you a little better.

CPD book club recommendation

Be Brilliant Every Day by Andy Cope and Andy Whittaker
(See bibliography)

Bloggers' corner

'5 steps to better school/community collaboration' by Brendan O'Keefe
Twitter handle: @insightguy
(Link in bibliography)

TO DO LIST:

- ☐ Understand the part that your school plays in the local community.
- ☐ Find out about the reputation of the school.
- ☐ Meet and speak to parents whenever the opportunity presents itself.
- ☐ Take all complaints and communication from residents as seriously as you would do from a parent.
- ☐ Make contact with significant local businesses.
- ☐ Open up effective channels of communication with significant religious or community groups.
- ☐ Invite representatives from local media outlets to get to know you and your school in more depth.
- ☐ Read *Being Brilliant Every Day* by Andy Cope and Andy Whittaker.
- ☐ Read '5 steps to better school/community collaboration' by Brendan O'Keefe.

12

Presence

Being successful in gaining your first leadership post is one thing, but being successful in leading school improvement is another. The following chapters explore how you can lead change in your school and be a highly successful school leader.

For many teachers, moving into senior leadership might also mean moving to a new school like we have discussed in previous chapters. If this is the case, you will find yourself having to build up your reputation as a leader from scratch. Whereas in your previous school you may have built this up over years and be a well-respected member of the team, in your new school this counts for nothing. All eyes will be on you in the first term as staff look to work you out and see what type of leader you really are. Equally if you have just secured an internal promotion in your existing school, your colleagues will be interested to see how you might transition from 'one of the gang' into 'one of them'.

In either of these two scenarios it is imperative to make it a priority to build up your reputation in the first few days and weeks of your job and begin to develop your presence around the school. The best leaders we find ourselves drawn to are leaders of people. These leaders are influential and inspirational in equal measures and manage this by being visible. No matter how busy you are, never underestimate getting out from behind your desk and walking the school. Being visible to both staff and students is absolutely key for every school leader, and the quicker you do it in your new role, the quicker you can start to regain that stock you once had in your old school or old role.

Presence also builds other people's confidence in you and your ability as a leader. Someone who is visibly supporting other colleagues and is prepared to stand shoulder to shoulder with colleagues in tough times, rather than hiding away behind their desk, is the type of leader that everyone would like to have. This style of leading from the front line is always well received by staff because they see someone who is prepared to roll up their sleeves and pitch in, rather than someone who is just happy to bark orders from the back.

Think about the leaders whom you have worked for in the past. What made you respect them, or lose respect for them? How did their presence, or lack of it, influence the type of feelings you had towards them and the general level of confidence that staff had in them?

Although developing your general presence has to be part of everything you do, day in and day out, there are some specific opportunities that you can use to further increase your presence as a school leader.

Learning walks

Whilst in some schools learning walks can be seen as the threatening side of senior leadership, the best senior leaders use this opportunity to support their staff. By regularly walking the school you can learn a lot about the quality of teaching and learning, student behaviour and standards, whilst also building up essential positive relationships with both staff and students. However, although best intentions tell you to walk the school as frequently as you can, once you get busy, this is usually the first thing to suffer. Therefore, it is vitally important that either your senior leadership team officially schedules these walks every week for all of the senior leaders, or you schedule your own in your diary so you don't forget.

In my time as a senior leader I've seen many approaches to learning walks, and the one thing I've learned more than anything is to ensure that staff feel supported and not observed. Even if you are not intending to observe anything or take any notes, if you walk around with a clipboard in your hand, you are signalling to everyone that this is not just a quick, informal 'pop your head round the door'. Although your presence will certainly be felt, this is not the type of presence you want to be known for in the early days of your role. My experience has taught me to leave the clipboard behind, walk into classrooms with a smile, address the teacher and ask how things are going, speak to a couple of students if the opportunity presents itself and then leave. A great tip that I picked up from my colleague Michael Laidler is to ensure that either you do or a fellow senior leader does a learning walk last lesson on a Friday. This is not necessarily to check up on the quality of teaching at the 11th hour of the week, but instead to get around as many classrooms as you can to wish people a good weekend. It's these little things that can make the biggest differences in senior leadership.

Walking the school in pairs is also a very good way of either building up your presence as a new senior leader or helping to build up somebody else's. The presence that a new member of staff can gain from walking the school with the headteacher can be huge in the early days of their role. This is also the same for a middle leader wanting to increase their presence, develop their skills and spread their wings a little. It can feel a little out of their jurisdiction or comfort zone to walk the school on their own, popping into classrooms and saying hello, but with a fellow senior leader with them, they can develop this without feeling that they are acting above their station. Walking in pairs also gives you the advantage of being able to talk about what you see in classrooms and discuss how this can either be shared as good practice or improved upon if required.

Walking the school with a colleague not only increases your presence, but also gives you the opportunity for quality discussion time, something that you can quickly lose if you are part of the 'I'm too busy club'. Many studies have shown that walking meetings are some of the most productive and produce some of the most creative ideas (e.g. Peck, 2016). Getting the oxygen flowing around your body whilst you are talking and thinking is said to be so much better than being hunched up over your desk. A great example of this is the approach that has been adopted by workers at LinkedIn's California headquarters. Here, staff regularly use the on-campus bike path as the perfect meeting place. The walk lasts approximately 25 minutes and staff believe that the informal nature of the walk helps break down formalities, and less eye contact helps staff be more open and honest with their colleagues. There's also the benefit of not being interrupted by the phone or a colleague from next door. No email alerts, no calls, no knocks at the door. I think we'd all settle for a meeting like that!

Duty

Although even the most cheerful of teachers will tell you otherwise, your weekly duty on your timetable isn't normally greeted with a fist pump of emotion! As a senior leader new to post though, this is another opportunity to get out and about. However, in my experience, and I'm sure you can all recognise what I'm about to describe, there are two very different approaches to doing a school duty. Firstly, there is the 'I don't want to be here' and the 'I trained to be a teacher, not a health and safety supervisor' attitude. These are the teachers and leaders who stand with their hands firmly inside the deep pockets of their oversized waterproof jacket and barely say a word or offer a smile to anyone. The quicker their duty is over, the better, and they are extremely skilled in standing or moving towards areas where students are well-behaved and quiet, rather than venturing into the lion's den. What these teachers and leaders miss is that every opportunity to be out of their classroom is an opportunity to develop their presence and relationships with both staff and students.

The second approach to duty is an approach where you consciously see this as a quick and easy opportunity to further develop relationships with the school community. Smiling and chatting to both staff and students in this informal and impromptu way is the perfect way to develop your presence. When you start to consciously view your duty as an opportunity to do this, rather than a waste of your precious planning and preparation time, you can then start to use it effectively. Rather than just standing in the spot that you were directed to, you will start to walk towards opportunities for conversation and begin to create opportunities where you can smile and enter into friendly dialogue with the people around you.

You must also remember that you don't only have to go out on duty on your specified, timetabled day. Think about the message it will send to someone if you tell them that you'll step in for their duty today as a random act of kindness. As a leader in the school, getting out to support others and show your face on even the coldest and wettest of days will certainly raise your stock in the staffroom. Not only will this be regarded positively by staff but, depending on when and where you stand, you can also start to develop relationships and respect with parents. Standing on the school gate in the morning is a great way to do this. Not only do you get the chance to greet your students with a smile every morning, but you also get the chance to say good morning to the parents who drop them off, letting them see you out on the front line of the school. Getting regularly noticed as being cheerful and welcoming to the students and, more importantly, to *their* child, can hardly be a bad thing. Never underestimate the power and positive message that this sends about you and your school. If you ever have to make a difficult phone call to one of these parents, they can never accuse you of not caring for their child or not looking out for them.

School events

Every school has a multitude of events going on throughout the year, from a Year 7 football match to the music department's Christmas concert. These events are usually optional for staff to attend, but as a new senior leader it is another great opportunity to show your face and, more importantly, show that you care about what is happening in the school. A quick glance at the school calendar will let you see most of the events that are coming up that term and you can begin to plan some of them into your own diary.

We all get to the stage where you could just do with going home at 5pm rather than staying for the art exhibition at 6.30pm, but if you are looking to develop your presence in the early stages of your senior leadership career, imagine the boost that the art department would get if you turned up to support them. This is even more important if you know you are having to make tough decisions around the school. Nobody can question your morals or your motives if they can clearly see that you are, above everything else, interested in the students' achievements.

Parents' evening is another great opportunity for you to utilise in developing your presence within the school. As a senior leader you may find that you have little or no appointments on some parents' evenings. Rather than seeing this as an early finish that day, the leader who is thinking about how to raise their profile with the parents of the school views this as another great opportunity. At parents' evening, lots of parents are usually stood around waiting for teachers to become free and some are looking at their maps trying to work out which teacher teaches their son or daughter. It doesn't take much effort to wander the room saying hello to parents and asking them how they are or if they need help finding someone. Although they may know your name as a new leader in the school, making a strong and polite first impression in person is priceless.

However, irrespective of which event you attend, you must remember that as a senior leader, you will be expected to answer questions and queries from parents about the content of the evening. Make sure you do your homework on the event and be ready to help parents by answering any questions they have. The good work you've done by being there can very quickly fade away if you can't help parents out.

Chapter 12 takeaway

Teaching tip

At the start of every year, make sure that you schedule your learning walks in your timetable and diary. This will ensure that you don't forget them or let them drop to the bottom of your to do list. It's also important to look at the whole-school calendar and put all of those events that you are required to attend in your diary. When events creep up on you and you haven't planned to be there, that's when it can cause you stress, both at school and in your personal life.

Pass it on

Developing your presence around the school is great, but if you can do it whilst being out there with a colleague, that's even better. The opportunity to create quality time with your colleagues in the corridors of the school or on the school playground is really important. This uninterrupted time can be some of the most valuable time in your working week.

CPD book club recommendation

Presence by Amy Cuddy
(See bibliography)

Bloggers' corner

'Visible leadership for better learning' by Owen Carter
Twitter handle: @od_carter
(Link in bibliography)

To do list:

- ☐ Get your leadership team to schedule regular learning walks around the school.
- ☐ Add your learning walks to your timetable as an immovable fixture.
- ☐ Get your hands on a copy of the whole-school calendar and look for important events throughout the school year.
- ☐ Add these events to your diary so they don't creep up on you.
- ☐ Look for opportunities to be out and about whenever and wherever you can.
- ☐ Read *Presence* by Amy Cuddy.
- ☐ Read 'Visible leadership for better learning' by Owen Carter.

13 Effective meetings

My experience has shown me that one of the biggest changes when moving from middle management into senior leadership is the amount of staff that you will now be leading. As a senior leader you can't do everything on your own and it's more about how you can articulate your vision to your teams and then ensure that you monitor, motivate and support them in making it happen. Meetings are therefore your conduit for doing this, so need to be seen as an essential part of your school improvement strategy rather than an inconvenience in your busy diary.

For some new senior leaders, this may be the first time that you've had to lead weekly meetings, especially one-to-one meetings with staff that you line manage. This can potentially be daunting, particularly if you are new to the school and find yourself having to line manage experienced staff. Leaders have to be strong, and neither ducking meetings nor letting your staff 'just get on with their jobs' are acceptable. Without your regular monitoring, motivation and support, you simply aren't leading anyone and they could quite happily keep on doing what they are doing with or without you. The very best leaders know exactly what their team are doing, how well they are doing it and what they need to do to be better at it.

These regular meetings and 'catch ups' can be either team meetings, individual one-to-one meetings or a combination of both. Depending on your context, the size of your team and the diverse nature of their roles, you'll need to find a balance that works for your school. Individual meetings are great for discreet and specific roles and are also the perfect place for holding people to account for their individual roles and responsibilities. Team meetings are great when people are working towards a shared goal and the nature of the conversations and agenda points cut across everyone's roles.

Preparation and planning

In order for meetings to be as effective as possible and not seen as a waste of everyone's time, they need to be planned. You should never walk into a meeting without pre-planning the content and what you want to achieve. The secret to effective meetings and your staff valuing them is to ensure they are as quick and as slick as possible, whilst also being productive. If you and your team feel that they have got something from a meeting and that it's been run in the smoothest and most efficient way possible, then they'll gladly turn up to the next one full of optimism and enthusiasm. Drag them out over hours and hours without getting anywhere and you can be sure that you'll create an atmosphere where your staff are so bored and fed up that you'll never come up with any good ideas or solutions.

The best way to plan for the content of meetings is to create an easy-to-access notepad or list that you can add ideas to throughout the week. By having something like this, you can add things when they happen or come to your mind, rather than having to try to think up an agenda just before a meeting. This way, the agenda is always full of essential discussion items. The best way I have found to do this is to use a simple 'to do' style app that you can add agenda items to, right from your smartphone. The best apps enable you to share and collaborate on lists with your staff so they can see the items that you are adding, meaning they can be prepared for the meeting just as you are. Having two people fully prepared for a meeting will almost certainly mean it will be far more productive with both people on the same page from the offset.

The cost of a meeting

When was the last time you stopped to take account of how many people were sitting around a meeting table and how much each of those people is paid per hour? When you break their salary down by week, by day and then by hour, you suddenly realise how much money is sitting around that table. Ask yourself the question: 'Have we just got £100/£500/£1,000 worth of value from that meeting?' With face-to-face time being so precious in school, especially trying to find a time in people's timetables to get everyone together in the same room, it's essential to start thinking like this about your meetings. If the answer to your question is 'no', 'hardly' or 'never', then you need to go back to the drawing board and start to think about why you are holding these meetings in the first place. One of the biggest hidden costs in school is human resources. Although you may not see the initial outlay of money on people's salary to hold a meeting, the cost is there. If they were not sitting in that meeting, they could be using their time to do something else, so make sure if you're asking them to sit in a room with you, that you are getting productivity from it.

Attention to detail

To the untrained eye, a meeting is where a group of people just enter a room and start talking, but behind the scenes there's been a lot of planning to make it run smoothly and attention has been paid to the slightest of details.

Agenda

Every effective meeting has an agenda as its backbone to ensure that you keep on track of what you said you'd be discussing. As previously mentioned in this chapter, the best way to formulate this agenda is as things come up through the week, rather than trying to force one together just for the sake of it. You should also give your team the opportunity to add or suggest items to be added to the agenda as well. However, it is important to have a final look at these before it goes live. Some items may not be appropriate for a team meeting and may be better off being added to their individual meeting with you. Once the agenda is finalised, send it out to whoever is invited to the meeting so that they can get their head around the items to be talked about and do their own homework and preparation before attending. If your meetings have a clear focus, there's far more chance of them being an effective use of everyone's time.

Standing items

You may want to have some standing items that are always on the agenda every week for your meetings. For individual meetings with the staff that you line manage this may be a list of their areas of responsibility. For a team meeting, it may be the big projects that you are undertaking as a team, your core values or school vision. Having these standing items on the agenda gives you the opportunity to always talk about them, check up on progress and not forget the key areas that you are holding people to account for.

Time of day

If you are lucky enough to be able to choose the time of day that you meet with your individual staff or teams, think carefully about what time will be most effective. Is a breakfast meeting better for all of you? Are you fresher and more creative at that time of day as opposed to the end of school after a full day at work? Whichever time you choose, make sure that it's not shoehorned into a small gap so it feels like it's always rushed. The worst time for this is break time. You need to remember that a meeting is not just about you speaking to your team. It's also an opportunity for them to speak to you, gain advice and bring problems to you. If they feel they are getting rushed out of the door, then they won't feel like it's a two-way street. The time you have with your staff, either individually or as a team, should feel like quality time to them, where they get your undivided attention.

Length of time

We've all been in meetings that run for two to three hours. Nobody looks forward to these and the energy and creativity in the room usually start to run dry after about 90 minutes. As a leader who is running the meeting, you need to be aware of this and control how much goes into your agenda. Irrespective of how important things are, if it's item number ten on a busy agenda, you probably won't get any quality discussion when it gets to that point anyway. Look to keep an end time in mind and think about the amount of time you are willing to give to each item. This will keep the focus on the meeting sharp and productive rather than getting sidetracked by idle chit chat.

Location

Choosing the right location for a meeting is also key to its success. The difference between your office and the school boardroom or conference facility can be quite significant. Depending on how formal or informal you want a meeting to be, the correct location can make all the difference. It's also worth thinking about the arrangement of the furniture. Sitting behind your desk for a meeting can seem quite formal, and there might be times when this is exactly what you want, whereas pulling up a chair next to someone can give quite the opposite message. These details should be thought about in the planning of the meeting, not as people walk through the door. The last thing you want is to be fumbling around with chairs and desks when they arrive. Know how you want the room and get it organised in advance.

Lead the meeting

As the senior leader, it is your job to lead the meeting and keep it on track. This may be the first time you've had to do this and it's quite a skill in itself. Every meeting needs someone to keep the team or participants on track by keeping one eye on the clock and the other eye on the agenda. The more skilled you get at this, the more you can detect when an item is going off on a tangent and when it needs to get pulled back on track. It's also your job to make sure the meeting sticks to the timeframe that you've given it and that items roughly take the amount of time that you have allocated for them. You don't want to cut an item off in mid-flow just because it's run over its allotted time, but if you start to sense that it's not going anywhere, then it's time to respectfully ask someone to wrap it up so you can move on. The same goes for knowing when to stop the meeting. Meetings that go on forever don't motivate anybody to contribute; instead people are consciously keeping quiet so it can get finished quicker. Some items might be best being rolled over to next week so that the meeting can end on time, giving quality time to those items next time. Nobody wants to feel that their important item has been brushed over in two minutes at the end of a meeting just because people wanted to get home.

Minutes

Having you or someone else take minutes of the meeting is an essential part of effective meetings. Although this can be tricky if it's just you and a member of staff in an individual meeting, it's something that shouldn't be overlooked.

Without an accurate account of what was discussed and what you have asked somebody to do and by when, you can't effectively or accurately hold them to account for their performance. I have found that typing quick notes into a pre-designed template on my computer during meetings is the quickest way to do this. I can then email them out afterwards so we both have a record of what was discussed and any action points. The minutes of the previous meeting should then be your starting point in every meeting. A quick look through the minutes will tell you what you agreed last time and what you were going to do. If this checklist becomes the norm in every meeting you have, holding your team to account for their performance against their responsibilities will become automatic.

Digital resources

When planning meetings for teams of people, printing off the necessary resources for certain items can increase the cost of your meetings significantly. Like I previously suggested in terms of counting the cost of the salaries in the room, start looking at the amount of paper that is printed and copied for your meetings. Then be honest with yourself, or even ask your team how often they look at those bits of paper afterwards. Is their filing cabinet just one-way storage where things go in but never come back out? Think about how you could do this differently by using digital resources. Can resources be emailed out in advance, thus reducing the need to print them?

Chapter 13 takeaway

Teaching tip

At various stages in the year (e.g. the last week before Christmas) it might be far more effective to cancel a meeting and give that time back to your staff so that they can get home early. If your staff appreciate that you are looking out for them and their wellbeing, you'll get it back in spades anyway. When things aren't urgent, sometimes it's better to put your effort into making people feel loved and looked after, rather than on their knees.

Pass it on

In the first few weeks of your new role, take the time to speak to your colleagues about how meetings have been run previously. You'll be able to pick up whether there is any resentment for meetings and how effectively (or not) they have been run. Using the 'quick wins' strategy from Chapter 9, if you make the changes immediately that everyone has been wishing for, then your stock will rise quicker than you can imagine.

CPD book club recommendation

Quiet Leadership by David Rock
(See bibliography)

Bloggers' corner

'Outstanding meetings: How groups drive improvement' by Dan Nicholls
Twitter handle: @DrDanNicholls
(Link in bibliography)

TO DO LIST:

☐ Find out who you are line managing.
☐ Decide how frequently you'd like to meet them, e.g. weekly, fortnightly, half-termly?
☐ Create the time and space in your timetable for your meetings and add them as immovable fixtures.
☐ Think about the locations of each meeting. Do you need to book a specific room in the school?
☐ Plan your meetings with specific attention to the detail that will make them highly effective.
☐ Read *Quiet Leadership* by David Rock.
☐ Read 'Outstanding meetings: How groups drive improvement' by Dan Nicholls.

14 Difficult conversations

Just as we discussed in the last chapter, being a senior leader is about leading the people who you line manage and holding them to account for their performance. In an ideal world, everyone would be great and perform in line with the targets that you set them, but as we all know, this is a tad unrealistic. With the very nature of the challenging targets that the government, Ofsted and we as school leaders set ourselves and our staff comes the reality that not everyone is going to achieve them. This is where your careful man-management of your human resources via the meetings that we discussed in Chapter 13 is so important. We must all remember that just because somebody has not achieved one of their aspirational performance-based targets, it doesn't mean they're not working as hard as they can. It can be too easy to just look at the numbers and not think about the person.

However, from time to time you will undoubtedly unearth issues that you are not happy with, which you feel have fallen below the expectations that you set out for the staff that you lead. To most of us this is hard to deal with in the first instance because of two things. Firstly, as human beings, the vast majority of us don't tend to like conflict; it's just not who we are. Therefore, having to tackle an issue of below-par performance with someone whom you work with isn't normally at the top of our list when we think about the things we like to do. Secondly, like anything else, this gets easier and better with practice. As a teacher or middle leader in your school, you might not have been put into the position where you have been tasked with having to have difficult conversations with your own colleagues.

Due to our natural sense to avoid conflict, it can initially be easy to want to duck these conversations. Let's face it: they are not nice, you don't look forward to having them and they are called 'difficult' conversations for a reason. However, whether you like it or not, this is now a key part of your job as a senior leader. If you can't hold people to account for their own performance then you'll not be able to meet your own performance targets that have been set for you. Put simply, if you can get everyone in your team (or the individuals that you line manage) to meet their targets, you'll almost automatically have hit yours.

In my experience, when you are thinking about whether to tackle an issue with a member of staff, use your own children (if you've got kids) as an example. Would you be happy if this was the standard of education that your own children were receiving? Is this good enough for them? If the answer to these questions is no, then you have a moral duty to act upon it, otherwise you are letting another parent down. Knowing about the issue but choosing to duck the conversation just means you are compliant with this happening in your school and that is weak leadership. If you don't tackle the situation, you are just part of the problem and this directly reflects on your own standards.

With every issue that you come across that will potentially result in a difficult conversation having to be had, think about it like this – no matter how hard it might be to deal with, it will be a whole lot harder to explain to a set of parents or your headteacher that you knew about it, but you were too weak to deal with it.

Preparation and planning

Just as with running an effective meeting (Chapter 13), the secret to success with a difficult conversation is in the prior preparation and planning. You can make the conversation significantly easier for both you to deliver and the recipient to hear if you take the time to think it over beforehand. Knee-jerk reactions to situations normally lead to 'very difficult' conversations. Rushing off to find someone to give them a piece of your mind before you've even stopped to process how the conversation might go, or what you want out of the conversation, is always a recipe for a human resources disaster.

Prior to any conversation that might prove to be a difficult one, take time to think about the following things:

Plan the conversation

It's very easy to go into a conversation with someone based on raw emotion and not really think about where you want the conversation to go. This will almost certainly lead to a conversation that you didn't want to get into. Think about a time when you have got into a heated conversation with someone over something they've done. You need to stay clear of these types of conversations and instead make sure you have thoroughly planned what you want to say. Without this careful thought and prior planning, the conversation can quite quickly go down a road that you don't want it to go down and away from the focus of what's right for the children of the school.

Know the desired outcome

Part of the planning process is to think about what you'd like the desired outcome of the conversation to be and how you're going to get there. This may seem obvious, but the outcome cannot simply be to end up giving someone a piece of your mind or telling them off. The conversation must end up leading somewhere so that if you have had to remind someone of their responsibilities in a formal manner, it leads to what they are now going to do to put it right. All too often difficult conversations are planned with what people want to say, but not what is going to happen next. The latter part is crucial to putting things right and moving on professionally.

How to start the meeting

Think back to the time when you first asked a girl or a boy at school out for a date. Those first few words were the hardest and it took an awful lot of planning in your head to get them right. The same goes for difficult conversations with staff. Those first few opening lines where you spell out why you are both in the meeting are absolutely crucial. If you seem nervous or unconfident, then a member of staff might use this to think you either don't have the conviction in what you are saying or are vulnerable to a counter-argument from them. Equally, a threatening manner from the offset can be the catalyst for an extremely volatile meeting. Think carefully about how you want to open the meeting and the exact words that you are going to use. This will be significantly different for a member of staff who is expecting the conversation, compared to somebody else who is blissfully unaware of what is about to unfold. Starting with 'This is never easy to broach with someone....' can show your human side in a situation.

Rehearse the meeting in your head

Consider all the different types of response that the person you are going to speak to might come back with. Hopefully, by knowing the staff you are speaking to, you will be able to pre-empt their response. Will they be upset, angry, aggressive, etc.? By thinking about and planning for all eventualities, it means that you shouldn't get caught on the back foot. Rehearsing your responses to these possible scenarios means that you can almost script your replies and not be shocked or surprised by any situation. It is vital that you stay in control of the meeting and focus on what you set out to achieve. People may try to use emotion as a tactic to sidetrack you or look for sympathy. A leader who has planned for all possible eventualities can stay focused on the task in hand, knowing that they have rehearsed this very scenario in their head before the meeting has even started.

Prepare some notes

Preparing some brief notes as part of your planning can be a very useful way to keep the meeting on track, especially if someone is purposely trying to sidetrack you. A set of bullet points beside you can be the perfect way to help you signpost where you want the meeting to go, making sure that you don't forget any important issues that you want to raise. This also enables you to keep things in a sequential order in the meeting, moving on from one issue to another, finally bringing it to a conclusion. Many meetings can start with the right intentions, but then lose focus quite quickly with either idle chit chat or a curve ball being thrown by the other person. By having some notes, you can always feel that you are in control of where the meeting is going by bringing someone back to the main focus of the conversation.

Remove the person from the situation

Difficult conversations are usually difficult because you are having to speak to someone who may be a trusted colleague or a close friend. However, you must always remember to focus on the issue or the facts and ensure that the conversation doesn't become an attack on their personal character. Removing the person from your thoughts and just concentrating on what has happened makes this significantly easier to deal with. Like we discussed at the start of this chapter, 'Would you be happy with this standard of education for your own children?' If the answer is no, then you have a duty to resolve the issue, irrespective of who is involved.

Performance-related

Some meetings and difficult conversations can end up feeling like someone is just trying to flex their muscles or assert their authority over you. Emotions can spill out and by the end of the meeting you just feel that you've had a telling off and that you've left the meeting feeling no further forward in what you are to do next. It's therefore essential to ensure that your conversation and the outcome that you want is performance-related. Always link your meetings back to somebody's objectives or targets so that it can never just be seen as a clash of personalities.

Time of day/week

Although a certain time of day may suit you and your diary, try to think about the impact of this on the person receiving the difficult conversation. There are certain points in the day and week that you should try to stay away from. For example, speaking to someone right at the start of the day or first thing on Monday morning could potentially put that person in a mood for the whole day/week. I don't think anybody wants to come to work and be on the receiving end of a difficult conversation the minute they walk in the door. On the other hand, think about the effect that a conversation at 3.30pm on a Friday or right before a holiday break can have on someone. Do you really want to send someone away for the weekend or for a week stewing on what you've said with no immediate way of putting it right? Picking the right time is crucial and it often means that you have to sit on the situation for a few hours or days (if it's not that urgent) until you feel the time is right.

Location

Just as picking the right time is essential, so is choosing the right location. No matter how urgent you feel a situation is, or how important it is for you to get it off your chest and off your to do list, you should never catch someone in the corridor to do it. Catching someone off-guard in a public place is the worst type of leadership and doesn't endear you to anyone. As we discussed in Chapter 13, think about the type of location that you want to use for the meeting. For some difficult conversations, using your own office can shift the balance of power too much onto your side and seem unfair. Equally, if you know that someone is going to be worried about the nature of the conversation, having it in the school boardroom or a designated meeting room might send them over the edge with worry. Either way, invite them to the meeting and give them the professional respect of being able to prepare for it, rather than trying to catch someone unaware. If it is a very difficult conversation then think about the possibility of having a neutral staff member present in the room to witness the conversation. Protect yourself.

Preserve the relationship

Irrespective of how difficult the conversation is, or what the issue was in the first place, you must remember that these people are your colleagues. The ability to be honest but preserve your professional relationship with them is absolutely key. The best way to do this is to always conclude the meeting by agreeing a clear way forward. This may involve a list of actions to be taken, or it may just be a reminder of their roles and responsibilities. Either way, both parties agreeing on the next steps means that there is no confusion going forward. You must also remember that this meeting will probably not have been a good experience for them and they may have been worrying about it for a while. Take the time to tell them that you understand this and then thank them for coming. A smile and a handshake usually shows that you are still human and still respect them as a person.

Chapter 14 takeaway

Teaching tip

Reflect on your own experiences of difficult conversations, both on the receiving end and also delivering them. When have they gone well and when haven't they? Why might this be? What factors may have contributed to this?

Pass it on

In lots of situations, the reason we have to have difficult conversations is because we have either not communicated our vision and expectations clearly enough or not regularly monitored the staff we have asked to carry these out. Talk to your staff, meet them regularly and schedule quality time with them so you can review how things are going.

CPD book club recommendation
Good to Great by Jim Collins
(See bibliography)

Bloggers' corner
'7 ways to manage difficult conversations' by Ross Morrison McGill
Twitter handle: @TeacherToolkit
(Link in bibliography)

TO DO LIST:

- ☐ Wait for an opportunity to arise that you are not happy with.
- ☐ Don't duck the conversation.
- ☐ Plan and prepare for the conversation with your desired outcome in mind.
- ☐ Read *Good to Great* by Jim Collins.
- ☐ Read '7 ways to manage difficult conversations' by Ross Morrison McGill.

15 Holding people to account

In my opinion, one of the biggest factors in raising standards in any organisation is high-level accountability. We only have to look at our schools over the last 20 to 30 years to see the impact of this. Gone are the days when if students didn't want to revise for their exams, it was up to them. These days, teachers and leaders in schools up and down the country are held accountable for the performance of their students against strict and challenging performance targets. The culture of accountability has certainly changed over time and, for the most part, students have benefitted, coming out with better results than they may have done if they were left to their own devices like some of us were.

I also hold the belief that, in the vast majority of cases, the reason that some schools have either failed or struggled over the last 20 years has been down to a lack of accountability at all levels within the school. As leaders, it is essential that we remember that we are funded by public money, so it is our job to ensure that we are holding people rigorously to account for their performance. Children only get one chance at schooling, so we need to make sure that the people who are responsible for their education are giving them the best possible passport in life. However, the problem in some schools has been that the leaders have not fully understood the difference between responsibility and accountability. In lots of cases of underperforming schools highlighted in Ofsted reports, leaders have designated people responsible for areas of school performance, but not accountable for it.

Take a look at the following statement and see if you can recognise any people, roles or situations that may fall into one or both of the categories from your own experiences:

> The main difference between responsibility and accountability is that responsibility can be shared while accountability cannot. Being accountable not only means being responsible for something but also ultimately being answerable for your actions. (www.diffen.com)

Accountability in practice

Although this may sound easy, in practice it can be very hard. In Chapter 14 we discussed difficult conversations and how hard they can be when they need to be with a close colleague or friend. This is exactly the same when it comes to holding someone to account. You must put all personal feelings aside and focus on the performance of that individual. Like we mentioned in Chapter 14, would you be happy with the performance of that individual if they were responsible for your own children's education? You must also ensure that the people you are holding to account know that they are accountable for their performance and not just responsible for that area of the school. It's easy to assume that people know this, but it isn't always the case. You must make absolutely clear that although people are responsible for delivering a high standard of education to your students, they are also accountable for their own and their students' performance.

Accountability at all levels is a culture and not just a phrase on a poster. It needs to permeate through the whole school and be just as relevant and meaningful to senior leaders as it is to NQTs and support staff. Ultimately, we are all funded by public money and we all have a job to do. If this culture isn't running through the school like a golden thread in everything you do, then problems start to occur. This usually happens when one of the following three things don't happen:

1. The leader does not communicate a clear vision. Staff are unsure as to what they are being asked to do and how it fits into the bigger picture of what they are being held accountable for. Clear targets are not formulated with staff and instead they are just created for them, sometimes without their knowledge.
2. Targets are not reviewed with members of staff midway through the year as a progress check to see if they are on track. Both staff and line managers are left feeling unclear about the progress being made (if any) towards their previously agreed targets. In many situations, this can lead to big and unwanted surprises at the end of the year.
3. Leaders are faced with tough decisions over staff who fail to meet their targets, so choose to duck the conversations in a bid to keep everyone happy. This creates a culture where targets are not worth the paper they are written on, or a culture of double standards, where some people are rigorously held to account and others not so.

This culture does not just happen overnight though. It takes a relentless drive from leaders at all levels to make it a priority of their leadership. Only then, when it is seen as a key improvement strategy by all, will it begin to be embedded in the day-to-day practice of the school. You must remember, though, that the key phrase in all this is 'at all levels'. There are not many (if any) schools out there where accountability at the senior leadership level isn't alive and kicking. The difference in high-performing schools, though, is that this is happening at all levels like previously mentioned. Take for example your heads of department or faculty. Each one of these middle leaders will be held accountable for the performance and results of their department/faculty by a senior leader in the school. This will usually consist of clear targets communicated by the leader and regular progress meetings looking at key performance indicators throughout the year. This is a clear example of the senior leader holding the head of department/faculty to account. But now ask yourself the same question of the head of department/faculty.

- Are they holding the TLR (teaching and learning responsibility) holders beneath them to the same level of accountability?
- Are they asking each post-holder to write a development plan in relation to their agreed targets?
- Do they meet with them regularly to focus on key performance indicators and ask them to produce evidence and data to demonstrate their progress?
- Or is it just a series of cosy chats over a coffee in the department office?

Having read this paragraph, you should now be able to reflect on whether you have true accountability at all levels in your school.

Building a culture of accountability at all levels

If you're still reading this chapter, I guess it's fair to say that you are probably in a position where you feel that you've got some work to do in building an accountability culture. If this is the case, then the following areas are the first steps that you can take as a leader and as a school in creating it.

Development or action plans

All staff in responsibility areas should have a development plan or action plan that clearly spells out what they are going to do in order to achieve the agreed targets that have been set. These plans should directly feed into the department/faculty or whole-school plan and be integral to its success. This should be exactly the same for a TLR holder (second in department) or a senior leader.

Regular progress checks

Just as it says on the tin: schedule regular progress meetings with post-holders and ask them for data and evidence that demonstrate progress towards their targets. Think yourself into an Ofsted inspector's mindset. Would they accept having the wool pulled over their eyes when there wasn't any evidence to support someone's argument? By regularly checking progress through a simple RAG rating process, both parties should be explicitly clear about the progress being made and the performance being displayed by the individual.

Revisit previous action points

In Chapter 13 we discussed starting meetings looking at the action points from the previous meetings. This is a crucial part of accountability. It is okay to set people challenging tasks in specified timeframes, but if you never go back and check if they have been done, and to what standard, then they were a waste of time in the first place. Every meeting should start with these action points as a basic checklist. Staff should know that there's no point turning up to a meeting without having completed their actions from the previous meeting, because it's always the first thing you are going to check.

Getting people on the bus

In a climate of rigorous accountability at all levels, and against a backdrop of ever-increasing targets, it can be easy for some staff to feel like they might want to look for an easier life somewhere else. It is therefore your job to get your staff 'on the bus' with you, so you can begin that journey towards school improvement together. Without this motivation from within the organisation, staff will only ever work so hard, usually significantly below their potential. Once they realise that rigorous accountability is here to stay, their lack of motivation will normally lead them to look elsewhere in search of that easier life. This may seem great for people you might want to get rid of, but for the highly-talented-but-unmotivated teachers and leaders in your school, this is a crime of leadership. As highly effective leaders, we create the weather in our schools and it's up to us to motivate our staff to want to get on that bus with us; it doesn't just happen by chance.

There are, however, many ways to get your staff on the bus, some of which will see them stay on there and some that will see them wanting to get off at the next stop. If you can create a climate where nobody wants to get off, then you are already halfway there.

Drag them kicking and screaming

Some staff just won't want to get on the bus, no matter how nice it looks to you and everyone else. These are the staff who would rather walk than ride because of their fear of change. However, the vast majority of them will secretly like the bus when they eventually get on it. You just need to get them there first.

Fear factor

If you have to use fear tactics and scaremongering to get people on the bus, then you can be sure that they'll probably get off at the first available stop. Having people work under fear of their leaders only goes so far. They'll do things out of necessity, but not out of love. You'll therefore never tap into their true potential this way.

Intrinsic motivation

Showing people the 'why' behind any of your ideas and strategies (as previously discussed in Chapter 10) is the best way to get people to truly believe in what you're doing. If you can get staff to believe in it and do things because of their moral purpose and because they believe it's the right thing to do, then you'll have them on the bus forever. If you put the time and effort into this type of motivation right at the beginning, you'll reap the rewards throughout the year.

Extrinsic motivation

The beauty of working with people is that we're all slightly different. We therefore need to appreciate that although you'd like everyone in your school to develop their own intrinsic motivation for getting on the bus, there'll be some asking you 'What's in it for me?' As we're not privately funded companies, we can't start throwing bonus payments around to get people to work harder. Research by Dan Pink in his book *Drive* (2011) also suggests that financial motivation is not the answer to our motivational problems. There are, however, lots of ways that you can incentivise high performance in your school and getting 'on the bus' without putting a monetary value on it. All you need to do is understand the individuals you are working with and find out what makes them tick.

Getting people in the right seats on the bus

Getting people on the bus with you is only half the battle. Arranging the people into the right seats will be your most important task. Having a highly motivated bunch of people is one thing, but getting them in the best positions in your school to enable them to be as successful as they can be is another thing. For new senior leaders joining a school this can sometimes be quite a challenge if a team of people are well established in their roles. However, on other occasions it might be just the tonic that an established team needs when they have been going through the motions or stuck in their comfort zones for too long. Either way, as a leader you are responsible for who undertakes the roles and responsibilities in your team. Just like a football manager is held to account for their results on the pitch, you need to find the best positions for your players to make your team perform to the best of their collective ability.

Chapter 15 takeaway

Teaching tip

Take the time to reflect on whether your school has a culture of accountability at all levels. What does the current picture look like? And what needs to happen to ensure that this culture is a golden thread through everything you do?

Pass it on

Model accountability practices to the staff who you lead and talk to them about the importance of it as a key school improvement strategy. Tell them that you expect them to do the same with the people they lead.

CPD book club recommendation

Bloomsbury CPD Library: Mentoring and Coaching by Marcella McCarthy (See bibliography)

Bloggers' corner

'10 tips on how to run a mid-year appraisal' by Paul Ainsworth
Twitter handle: @pkainsworth
(Link in bibliography)

TO DO LIST:

- ☐ Get people on the bus.
- ☐ Get people in the right seats on the bus.
- ☐ Communicate clear targets related to your vision for school improvement.
- ☐ Regularly check progress against agreed targets.
- ☐ Read *Mentoring and Coaching* by Marcella McCarthy.
- ☐ Read '10 tips on how to run a mid-year appraisal' by Paul Ainsworth.

16 Leading change

Great leaders are not just good at leading an organisation that is already running smoothly. What really makes a leader great is the ability to influence positive change within a school to bring about school improvement and raise standards. Anybody can sit in the staffroom or their office and blame people below them, around them and above them for the problems in their school. The difference is that great leaders take action and refuse to accept poor standards of provision for the students in their care. They have a relentless drive to bring about change, irrespective of how hard that change might be to accomplish. Moaning about something in your school without doing anything about it only fosters a negative and defeatist attitude. If you're looking from the outside in, then all you see is a leader who is part of the problem and not either willing or capable of being part of the solution.

In many cases, new senior leaders are specifically brought into schools to do just that – bring about positive change. However, in my experience, I have found that although you may have been told what the issues are, you need to see them with your own eyes. If you are relying on information from someone who might be part of the problem, then you may only be getting half the story. In order to establish exactly what is happening and where your focus needs to be, you need to set aside some time in the first few days and weeks of your new role to effectively audit the quality of provision for yourself (however, this isn't always easy with limited time and the pressure of rapid improvement). You can then use this to either back up the information that you had been given previously or challenge it, based on your own judgement that you have been able to form.

Leading change isn't easy though. If it was easy, there wouldn't be an underperforming school in the world. Research from Ken Blanchard backs this up by estimating that as many as 70% of change projects fail in some way (2008). His research states that the reason that the intended outcomes of the project aren't met is usually down to it either not being implemented effectively or not being sustained. Although every school and every situation that requires leading some form of change is going to be slightly different, there are some key principles that should not be overlooked if you want it to be successful.

Accept the need for change

Once the need for change has been identified by either yourself or the headteacher, it needs to be carefully and effectively communicated to the wider school community. Depending on what that change may be, you will need to begin the process with key individuals. Any process of change that is not accepted by the wider school as being required will almost certainly fail. This is especially important to recognise when you are going into a new school to implement change. Many of the existing staff may not feel the need to change (they have been part of the problem for too long), so your first job needs to be to make people understand that there is a need for change. There are many ways to do this, depending on the size and context of the school, but almost all of the ways centre around actually speaking to people face to face. If you're not up for personally selling the need for change and being prepared to answer questions and challenge opinions, then you're probably not going to lead that change successfully. Simply sending a string of faceless emails and hiding behind new policy documents is not leadership.

Sell the 'why'

As previously mentioned in Chapter 10, part of selling the need for change comes from showing people the 'why'. Most people will want to support a new senior member of staff in their school and will do most of what you ask just out of obedience. However, true acceptance of change comes from when people understand it and then believe in it, rather than just doing it because you've asked them. When times get tough and people become tired, they will stop doing the things you want them to unless they can clearly see why they are doing it. Once you've successfully got people on board by accepting the need for change by understanding the 'why', then – and only then – can you begin to spell out the way forward.

Direction

Getting people to accept the need for change is one thing, but mapping out a clear direction for how you're going to bring about positive change is another. It's the easiest thing in the world to identify that something isn't working and then tell people that they need to perform better. Most of us do this every weekend when we watch a game of football. The skill we need to master as leaders is what happens next. Which direction are we going to go in and how are we going to get there? We talked about developing and communicating your vision in Chapter 9 and this is where it really comes into play. A leader without a vision is like a driver without a map.

A common mistake at this point is to rush into the direction without spending enough time planning and considering all of your options. You'll no doubt be excited to get going and will want to make some of those 'quick wins' that we also described in Chapter 9, but the last thing you want to do in a new role is set off on a hastily decided direction, only to find that you hit a dead end. Telling everyone that something is wrong and then publicly failing with your plan to fix it will do nothing to create confidence in your ability to lead change. All that will happen is that you'll have an even harder job to do when you ask for their buy-in on your next plan.

Teaching and learning at the heart of school improvement

We must always remember what our core business is – high-quality teaching and learning in our classrooms every hour, every day. Whenever you are planning for school improvement strategies and preparing to lead change in your school, you must always ask yourself if it's going to have an impact on the quality of teaching and learning. You can do all the work you want around the edges of your school on various school improvement strategies, but if it isn't having an impact in the classroom, then you're not going to be moving forward as quickly as you'd like or, in some cases, at all.

Many leaders make the mistake of adopting a sticky-plaster approach to school improvement and put significant time, money and energy into papering over the cracks created by poor teaching. Although this is fine in the immediate term as an intervention, it should never be seen as a long-term strategy for school improvement. The easiest, cheapest and most sustainable way to bring about change is by focusing on what is happening in the classrooms of your school every day and committing to raising the standard of teaching and learning.

Blockers

As creatures of habit, most of us don't like change and will tend to resist it unless we're absolutely sure it's going to be for the good. You'll also find that irrespective of how well you think you've done in speaking to people and selling the 'why', you'll still have a small group of staff who are out to block your plans for change. Some staff may feel they don't need to change and have seen change come and go before, whilst others may be fighting against the system due to individual grievances that they may have with the senior leadership of the school. Whatever their reasons, you just need to know who they are so that you can plan a strategy for how to win them over. With some people, you can do this overnight by going to speak to them personally, but with others you need to play the long game. Just don't expect everyone to be with you from day one. If you are ready and prepared to have to play the long game with some staff, then it won't feel like a setback when not everyone is jumping for joy at the thought of change.

Pre-mortem

We know from the earlier reference in this chapter to the research by Ken Blanchard that nearly 70% of change projects fail due to poor implementation. A technique that I picked up a few years ago from a TED Talk by Daniel Levitin ('How to stay calm when you know you'll be stressed', 2015) is the idea of conducting a pre-mortem in the planning stages of any change management project. In a pre-mortem, you simply either write down or discuss with your team all the possible things that could go wrong, or might stop your project from being successful. By doing this you are giving your team licence to be negative, something that they might not have naturally wanted to do with you as a new leader. Without this permission, people just agree with you because they don't want to be seen as trying to derail your plans, when in fact what you need is their honest input. With a thorough pre-mortem you can get rid of any negative thoughts people may have, look at every possible issue that may arise, and then work out a plan for how you are going to overcome them.

Developing influence in others

You may be good, but you're not going to make sizeable whole-school change happen on your own. You need to utilise your team and the human resources at your disposal, whilst also appreciating that there may be people in the school better placed than you to help make this happen. Being able to develop your influence through others is a key strength of a highly effective leader. Knowing that someone else in the school (irrespective of their level) can be a better agent for change than yourself can begin to open up so many more opportunities for change to happen. Identifying key staff who may have strong characters or influential voices is an effective way to reach corners of the staffroom that you can't. Once you've got these people firmly on your side, you can use them to subconsciously drip feed some of your messages and vision to others. Never underestimate the power and influence that they may have over others. If you can harness your own influence, together with theirs, you'll have more people clambering to get on your bus!

Keep it simple

As a rule of thumb, the more complex a plan is, the higher the chance of it not being successful. If staff don't understand it, or forget the complex detail, then they can't implement it. The best strategies in any organisation are simple to implement and therefore highly effective. When you're planning for change, think about the following concepts:

Simplicity

Real sophistication is the ability to do something simple really well. By keeping your strategies simple, it means that more people will understand it and when the going gets tough, people can still easily implement it. Don't be lured into thinking that you have to make a plan complicated to demonstrate your intelligence. It's actually quite the opposite. The ability to strip away all of the unnecessary actions, processes and red tape around a plan is where intelligence really comes into play.

Marginal gains

Sir Dave Brailsford, former Performance Director at British Cycling, championed the marginal gains strategy that was the foundation behind so many Olympic and World Championships cycling gold medals for Team GB. Instead of looking for silver bullets, the marginal gains approach is all about making small performance improvements in a number of areas. Once added together, these small differences make significant performance improvements, the like of which one single change could not come close to achieving.

Sustainability

The other key factor that Ken Blanchard found in change projects not being successful, other than poor implementation, was a lack of sustainability. Speak to any teacher in any school and they'll tell you about dozens of strategies that they've had to implement that were important for a few weeks, but then just faded away into the background after the initial honeymoon period. It goes without saying that any significant need for whole-school change needs to be committed to in the long term and not just become a flash in the pan. It is therefore vitally important that in your planning stage you think about how sustainable your plan actually is. Does it require constant sources of funding? Or is it heavy on staff time and energy? We've all seen strategies that work when Ofsted are in the building, but some of those are too labour-intensive to be sustained all year round.

The other way to ensure that your plan has a sustained level of commitment to it throughout the year is to make it a focus of departmental/faculty meetings. As a school, if you want to commit to something, then it has to be everyone's business, not just the leader's. Including it as a standing agenda item within these meetings means that it will not be forgotten when people get too busy. If people know that it's important enough to be included as a standing agenda item, they're more likely to put the necessary time and effort into it in the classroom, as opposed to a strategy that they know won't be around for long.

Chapter 16 takeaway

Teaching tip

Think about your experience of being on the receiving end of whole-school strategies that haven't proved to be successful. Why was this? Was there anything from the principles that we have discussed that the leader missed out on implementing? What could they have done differently to make that specific plan more effective?

Pass it on

By talking to colleagues about your vision and the 'why' you can increase your influence via other people. If you can get them 'on the bus' with you, they will be your best advocates for change and help fill the bus seats!

CPD book club recommendation

Much Promise by Barnaby Lemon
(See bibliography)

Bloggers' corner

'6 lessons for leading change in schools' by Battelle for Kids
(Link in bibliography)

TO DO LIST:

- [ ] Identify a need for change.
- [ ] Get people to accept the need for change.
- [ ] Sell the 'why'.
- [ ] Establish the direction.
- [ ] Keep teaching and learning at the heart of any plans for school improvement.
- [ ] Identify your blockers and conduct a pre-mortem.
- [ ] Keep it simple and commit to it.
- [ ] Read *Much Promise* by Barnaby Lemon.
- [ ] Read '6 lessons for leading change in schools' by Battelle for Kids.

17 Recruitment of high-quality staff

You'll soon work out that if you're not moving forwards, then you'll be going backwards. The following chapters look at how you can enjoy senior leadership, whilst constantly learning and striving to be better in an ever-changing educational landscape.

In any school or organisation, leaders must understand that human resources are their most expensive and best asset. This is even more important in the current educational climate we find ourselves in. The teacher recruitment crisis has been the nemesis of headteachers and senior leaders up and down the country for too long now, and in some schools it's having a significant negative effect on children. Ask any senior leader in any school and they'll be able to tell you some of the struggles they've had just getting a body in front of their kids, never mind a quality one. However, as we discussed in the last chapter, if you just moan about the way it is and don't do anything to change it, then you're just another part of the problem. Great leaders bring about change. They identify an issue and then work out how to positively impact upon it.

Although a national shortage of teachers joining the profession is clearly an issue, there are ways to at least recruit the best of what is out there. This starts with a commitment from all senior leaders in the school that recruitment and retention are everyone's responsibility. If you're lucky enough to work in a school with an HR team, they will certainly help and take their fair share of the administrative side of recruitment from you, but the strategic leadership of recruitment must come from you. Leadership teams that believe they are too busy to waste their time thinking about recruitment strategies are probably the ones that are running around trying to solve issues that have resulted from poor-quality staffing. My experience tells me that it's a lot cheaper to spend time and money on getting the right person in the first place than having to spend hours and hours of time trying to work with them afterwards when they are failing to meet the standards that you expect.

Leaders at all levels need to think about what they can do to attract the very best teachers. Gone are the days when you can just put out an advert and expect to be inundated with applications. With a lack of teachers in the recruitment pool to begin with, coupled with a significantly increased number of schools looking to recruit, it's a competitive market out there. You need to think about how you can market yourself to prospective candidates, not the other way around. The best schools and leaders have already mastered this and are recruiting well because of it. For others, it calls on a shift in mentality and a sharper focus on the fact that more time spent on recruitment might save time, money and energy further down the line.

Marketing

Marketing your school and the vacancies that you have is a key component in any successful recruitment campaign. If you're not careful, this can also be an extremely expensive exercise, with national advertising through mediums like the *TES* costing in the thousands. This is sometimes what puts schools off doing a lot of marketing for their vacancies. However, marketing doesn't always have to be an expensive game. There are many ways to be innovative with your marketing strategies, and more often than not, these cost-effective ways can sometimes be the most effective in terms of their impact. Let's look at the essentials, together with some innovative ways to make recruitment more effective.

The advert

Take a look at any advert you have put out as a school over the past 12 months. What does it say about your school and the type of school it is to work in? Is it any different to hundreds of other adverts that are posted every week by schools up and down the country? How can you make it stand out from the crowd with the type of information that you'd be looking for as a potential candidate? If your advert is going to be posted digitally somewhere (e.g. on your website), how can you include rich media in it so that it grabs someone's attention? A short video message from the headteacher about the role and what an amazing school it is to work in might just be the bit of magic you've been missing.

Local vs. national advertising

Depending on the position you are advertising, you'll need to decide on whether to advertise locally or nationally. As mentioned previously, the cost will significantly rise if you choose to advertise nationally in something like the *TES*, but you may feel that it's a cost worth committing to. Some teachers who are looking for new opportunities or promotions will only ever look in the national press for school vacancies, so it's worth bearing that in mind. However, that doesn't mean you can't be innovative in your local advertising. There are many alternatives to the traditional approach of just using the *TES*. As a leader, you should be exploring all the different options that are available to you. If you're not sure where to start, arrange to speak to a recruitment company (not necessarily linked to education) so that you can get into the mind of a recruitment expert.

Social media

There once was a time where websites were seen as being king. Putting an advert on your website was your answer to cost-effective marketing. However, that time has been overtaken by the rapid growth and impact of social media. Businesses and organisations across the world are now turning to social media as their go-to vehicle for global advertising. Websites are a great place to store the advert and links to download further content, etc., but social media is the vehicle that can get it seen by a much wider audience. Once it's liked, shared or retweeted on platforms such as Facebook, Twitter and LinkedIn, the potential viewing figures start to snowball.

The pack

If you're applying for a number of jobs at the same time, you'll no doubt receive a job information pack from a number of different schools. Think about the last one you received or gave out as a school. What did it really say about the type of school you are? The pack is the first opportunity you have as a school to 'wow' your potential applicant into wanting to work at your school above any others. I've witnessed first-hand when applying for jobs packs with typos, out-of-date information and general errors all over them. Is this the type of school that you'd want to represent? A great way to start this process is to select a few jobs that are currently in the press and ask for their application pack to be sent to you. Once you've received a range of them, compare your pack to theirs. How can you make yours stand out against the rest?

Unique selling point

For any of the above marketing strategies, you need to work out what your USP (unique selling point) as a school is. You may have a new building, great results, national accolades, etc. Irrespective of what it is, you need to sell it. Ask yourself and your SLT the question 'Why would someone want to come and work here if it wasn't for a promotion?' For some schools in competitive or challenging contexts, this might be difficult to work out. However, you need to find something that is going to draw staff towards the school. Once you've got your USP (or multiple USPs), make sure that they are prioritised in your various marketing strategies so that they come through loud and clear to any potential candidates.

Positive news

Prospective candidates will try to find out information about your school on the internet. A quick search will throw up a multitude of stories, some of which you might be happy with, some you might not. However, until you perform this search yourself, you won't know what stories they'll find. What does a search say about your school? And how can you generate more positive news stories that appear further up the search rankings in a simple Google search?

Staff as advocates

Your staff can be the best advocates for your school. If you are looking to work at a school, what better advert than seeing people who work there constantly sharing good news stories about the place? Ask your staff to share and repost your school social media articles as this generates a sense of pride in the school. When you've then got job adverts and vacancies to share, staff can help by sharing these on their own social networks, thus widening the reach of the posts, but also with the added authenticity of people who actually work there. Teachers always know other teachers, so you may just find that you pick up lots of interest in your jobs this way.

The interview

We have already discussed what to look out for in terms of senior leadership interview tasks in Chapter 6. The emphasis on such days is to put you under pressure and see how you perform in a multitude of diverse tasks. So how can we use the lessons we learned in that chapter to create more meaningful classroom teacher interviews that aim to tell us a bit more about the person we are potentially about to invest in? Think for a minute about the interviews that happen at your school. Are they any different from the structure of interviews that was in place ten or 15 years ago? If we know the profession has changed significantly in the last 15 years, then shouldn't our assessment of teachers looking to work in your school reflect that?

There is no hard and fast rule of which tasks you should make people complete, but review what you are currently doing and see if there's any way to make it better. You can put people off the job by going way over the top with a boot-camp-style day; getting the balance is key. If they are just sitting in your staffroom for hours between tasks, waiting for their interview slot, that is wasted time that you could be using to assess their abilities in other areas. Take a look at the following suggestions for interview day tasks and see if any of them are worthwhile adding to your existing template:

- **Lesson reflection** – Although teaching a lesson is fairly standard practice in a teaching interview, how about getting them to watch a pre-recorded lesson and give feedback to you on the strengths and development points of that teacher? Irrespective of the experience of the member of staff you are interviewing (NQT up to senior leader), if they deconstruct the performance of a teacher, they are far more likely to be a reflective practitioner who can take on board advice and guidance throughout their career.

- **Examination paper** – How well do they really know their subject? Why not get them to answer a series of questions from last year's GCSE paper? Or ask them to write a model answer that could be used as a teaching resource when thinking about how to answer a certain GCSE question? The great thing about this is that they can be doing this task between their other more practical tasks, whilst in the staffroom or your holding base.
- **Marking and feedback** – Having some work photocopied and ready to mark is a great way to see what they will be like in the role. Asking them to feed back to a group of students on their work enables you to see the quality of feedback that you'd get from them. You can also easily compare and contrast this with other candidates on the day and also other members of your current department/faculty.

Analysis of recruitment

One area of recruitment that is commonly missed in schools is the ability to analyse how successful a recruitment campaign has been. For most people this just means 'did we fill the vacancy?', but for forward-thinking schools who understand the importance of recruitment, as we have discussed in this chapter already, it's much more than that. As a starting point, why not look at the following two areas that might unearth some interesting findings about how well you recruit?

- **Where did they see the advert?** A simple one to achieve by just adding a list of options to a form, or asking the candidates when they come to interview. Lots of schools may already do this, but how many schools share this information with their senior leaders so that they can do more of the advertising that works? Do you know in your school where the most-seen adverts were for the last few jobs that you posted? Once you know this, you can start focusing your time and attention on the areas of marketing that yield the most impact.
- **Longevity** – Although you may feel that as an interview panel you've been successful because you've appointed someone, how do you know how successful that appointment will be in the long term? Are there certain people in your recruitment process that seem to always appoint poor choices? If you aren't doing any type of tracking exercise, then you'll never be able to put your finger on this. By creating a record or a spreadsheet that details all of your appointments, together with the names of the staff on your interview panel, you can go back over a series of years and track how successful that appointment was.

Chapter 17 takeaway

Teaching tip

Take the time to reflect on the current recruitment processes at your school. Do you invest enough time and energy in them? Could they be improved? Think also about the quality of people that you have employed recently. Are they outstanding practitioners? If not, what are the reasons behind this?

Pass it on

Everyone who works at your school will have been through some type of recruitment process, either at your school or another. Talk to people about their experiences of being on the other side of the process. Where do they look for job adverts? What would entice them to apply for another job at another school?

CPD book club recommendation

How to Survive in Teaching by Dr Emma Kell
(See bibliography)

Bloggers' corner

'Teacher turnover. Part of life' by Tom Sherrington
Twitter handle: @teacherhead
(Link in bibliography)

TO DO LIST:

- ☐ Review the current recruitment processes in your school.
- ☐ Think innovatively about how to market your vacancies.
- ☐ Understand what your USP is.
- ☐ Review and improve your interview day tasks.
- ☐ Start to analyse the success rates of each of your recruitment campaigns.
- ☐ Read *How to Survive in Teaching* by Dr Emma Kell.
- ☐ Read 'Teacher turnover. Part of life' by Tom Sherrington.

18 Retention, development and wellbeing

Once you've recruited the best staff you possibly can, your next job is to make sure that you can retain them. It's disappointing to invest all that time, effort and money into recruiting them, only for them to leave within a couple of years because of the conditions and environment within your school. Of course you'll have staff leaving for promotions if there are no such opportunities available at your school, but the very best schools, who understand the value of their staff and the environment that they work in, shouldn't be losing people to sideways positions in neighbouring schools. The leaders in these schools understand that their human resources are their biggest and best asset, and work hard to understand the needs of each and every one of their staff, so that they can keep an entire workforce happy. Ask any leader in any organisation or business on the planet and they'll tell you that a happy workforce, who understand what and why they are doing what they do, will normally lead to better performance.

A common misconception that lots of people make, though, is that happiness is always intrinsically linked to financial rewards. Don't get me wrong, more money is always going to make people smile and say thank you, but that's not why most people came into the profession. If we were all motivated by cash incentives, then we'd have left the profession long ago and started chasing sales-target-style jobs that offer cash bonuses in return for meeting specific targets. In fact, research by Daniel Pink, in his book *Drive* and his engaging TED Talk about motivation, suggests that financial rewards often have a negative effect on performance measures, creating a tunnel-vision approach to finding solutions, rather than a more creative and open-minded approach, which is what most educational problems require (2011). Schools also have increasingly tight staffing budgets that prohibit you from just throwing money at people to stay. It might be the first thing on your mind to offer someone a TLR payment just to stay, but how is that going to work in the long term? Can you sustain that type of staffing structure in your budget? What happens when someone else finds out that you effectively paid someone to stay?

Speak to most people in your school, or any friends in the profession, and they'll tell you a different story about why they love their job or the school that they work in. Common reasons are usually linked to job satisfaction, feeling valued and supported, the level of personal and professional development that they receive, together with just loving what they came into the profession to do – teach children. Money is very rarely mentioned. Work out what motivates people and why they love doing their job, and then give them more opportunities to feel it, see it and do it. If you get this right, you'll have more and more staff enjoying where they work and far fewer staff interested in jumping ship. If you build your reputation as a school for watering the grass on your side of the fence, then people will always want to flock to and stay on the lovely green grass that you cultivate.

Workforce

The leadership of human resources can scare lots of people off and for some leaders they think it's just something that the headteacher or the HR department need to worry about. However, anyone responsible for leading a team of people needs to be aware that they play a hugely significant role in human resources and that the principles of creating a happy workforce are not that complicated to master.

Make staff feel valued

Nobody wants to work in a school, a business or an organisation that doesn't value their staff. This sounds simple, but how you do it is another thing altogether. Virtually every leader in every school will tell you that they value their staff and the teams that they lead, but ask the staff or the teams underneath them if they agree with this and they may give you a different answer. If this is the case, then a question needs to be asked about what the leaders do to overtly and explicitly show their teams that they are valued. Ask yourself the very same question: 'When was the last time that you took time to personally thank someone for their contributions, thoughts or actions in a way that affectionately demonstrated that you valued them as a person and a professional, not just the latter?' It's easy to send an email or stand up and say a blanket 'thank you' to staff in briefing or a whole-staff meeting, but the difference that actually going out of your way to speak to someone makes is huge.

Staff development

Making people feel developed, both personally and professionally, is absolutely key in creating a climate of job satisfaction. This is even more important when you are dealing with education professionals. If their job is to be responsible for developing people into being a better person each and every day, then it's only natural to want to feel the same development over time yourself. If you feel that a school is improving you as a person and as a professional, then that normally leads to personal satisfaction. Some schools are wary of developing staff too well in case they leave for promotion. However, a great quote I saw from David Weston, Chief Executive at the Teacher Development Trust, sums it up: 'What if we develop our staff and they leave for promotion? What if we don't develop them and they stay?' A great example of this comes from what my old headteacher Steve Harness used to call 'Butterfly Projects'. These small 'non-payment' projects were given to up-and-coming staff so that they could spread their wings a little and get a flavour for whole-school development projects.

Climate for development

Although you may have prioritised the development of your staff, you can only be successful in doing this if you have created the right climate in your school. Leaders need to create a climate where every person in the school building (irrespective of age) wants to make themselves a better person. Once you can get your staff away from sitting and moaning in the staffroom at lunchtime and, instead, get them excited about a new strategy they have tried or a resource that has worked, then you can really start to go places. This culture of learning, and the idea that everyone is a learner, will begin to permeate through everything you do. If people are excited about what they are doing and enthused by it, then it will always end up having an impact in the classroom. Getting to this utopia can be difficult though, as there are no silver bullets or magic tickets to get you there. It takes time and a commitment to the little things that make the biggest differences. For example, spend a little bit of money on some high-quality teaching books and create a reading club where people swap books and share their experiences of what they've read. This way you are demonstrating you are valuing their development by purchasing the books for them, but creating a climate where people can come together, discuss what they've read and work out how to implement it in their classrooms.

Listen to staff

One of the things we don't do enough of, due to the fast-paced nature of life in our schools, is take the time to listen to our staff. However, if leaders prioritised this a little more in their day-to-day roles, they might be able to find out all of the answers to the above three areas. It's crazy to think that schools spend huge proportions of time thinking about how to keep staff happy without actually speaking to them and asking their views. This is also true for when staff are moving on from your school. The best and most honest feedback you can get about what it's like to work at your school can come from conducting exit interviews. When people are leaving they are always more inclined to be honest about the school. You may just find that taking the time to sit down and have a proper conversation with someone about why they are leaving will save you from losing the next three or four staff members who are fed up about the same issue. Once you know about it, you can then do something about it.

Wellbeing

One of the biggest problems that leaders are facing in terms of trying to retain high-quality staff is people leaving the profession due to workload and wellbeing. National statistics continue to demonstrate that the number of teachers leaving the profession prior to retirement age is increasing (DfE, 2017), even though the amount of money that the government is spending on teacher training is also increasing. It is therefore essential that as leaders we do everything we possibly can to look after the wellbeing of our staff so that they can perform to the best of their abilities every day in their classroom. Would you want your own children to be taught by teachers who were stressed out, couldn't sleep and didn't have the energy to plan and deliver exciting lessons?

Physical wellbeing

This doesn't just apply to teachers either. As school leaders we are charged with making big decisions about the direction of our schools and those decisions require us to be fresh and in a good state of mental wellbeing. Being constantly 'on' and thinking about our schools 24/7 only makes us mentally fatigued and unable to make sound decisions. How many times have we seen poor decisions made either in our schools or on a sports field when the brains and bodies of the decision-makers are fatigued? Although we sometimes feel that we need to keep going and tough it out, how good are we to our school if we are only ever running at 70 per cent? Would you ever see a professional athlete constantly performing at their best without regular rest and recovery? Do they train and perform night and day, every day, still expecting the very best outcomes? If we start to think of ourselves as the educational versions of professional athletes, the people at the cutting edge of our industry, then we might start to think about the conditions in which we can perform at our very best. Are we getting enough rest and sleep to let our body recover each day? Are we allowing our brain to switch off from the mental demands of our schools? Are we getting enough 'down time' away from our jobs in the company of our family and loved ones?

If you're not allowing your batteries to recharge away from school and you're saying that you don't have time for all that stuff due to the nature of your job, are you really giving 100 per cent to your school? Or are you just giving 100 per cent of the 70 per cent you have left in the tank?

Practical wellbeing

One thing is sure in terms of wellbeing, there is no medal for being the last one out of the building. In this day and age with digital technology and remote access to documents via cloud services, most of a teacher's marking, planning and preparation can be done at home. A good leader who is looking out for the wellbeing of his or her staff should then appreciate that this work does not have to be done in the school building and that everyone's personal circumstances are different. Some staff may find it easier to stay at school and get their marking and planning done before they leave so that their family time is sacrosanct, whereas other staff may feel that getting home early to see their children is vitally important and their school work can be done after their children go to bed. Either way, great leaders need to remember that there is no 'one-size-fits-all' approach to the personal organisation of a teacher's workload and that everyone should be able to find their own way to achieve a healthy work–life balance.

Digital wellbeing

With the rapid development of modern technology, it can become too easy and tempting to check your email, reply to the odd message on your phone and even be tempted into remotely logging into your desktop from the comfort of your own home to complete those tasks that simply can't wait until you're back at your desk. The irresistible need to be 'always on' has been fuelled in recent years by advances in modern technology, enabling communication to be so much more accessible and instantaneous. In many ways this has been a significant shift in how we communicate and has increased our productivity as teams in schools monumentally. Our communication is now unrecognisable from what it was when I entered the profession, but so, unfortunately, are the demands on us during our 'out-of-hours' time.

Evenings and weekends are now regularly punctuated by the sound of an incoming email from school that you feel you must reply to immediately. The knowledge that everyone knows you get your emails on your phone can make you feel powerless to not reply during your leisure time for the fear that you may be seen as not as committed to the cause as everyone else. Even when you make the stance to not reply straight away and leave it in your inbox, you sometimes get that text message saying, 'Did you not get my message?' And for some couples, what was historically marked on the weekly calendar as 'Date Night' has now turned into 'Data Night', pouring over an Excel spreadsheet rather than a movie.

Unless leaders across the country take a stand against this digital intrusion on our personal lives, we may find that the boundaries between our professional time at work and our personal time at home are blurred so significantly that people burn out mentally as well as physically. Although you may have staff who want to answer emails and work during evenings and weekends, you must just be aware that not everyone will. Somebody sending an email after the traditional hours should not expect a response until the next working day and there should be no pressure exerted to reply to it.

Chapter 18 takeaway

Teaching tip

Think about what used to annoy and frustrate you earlier in your career. Would any of those things annoy and frustrate the people in your team? Are there things in your power that you can do to make people feel more valued, developed or happy at school?

Pass it on

When was the last time you asked your team what they value at school and what would make their jobs even more enjoyable or satisfying? By opening up this dialogue, you may be able to create an even more productive and satisfying environment at school.

CPD book club recommendation

Leading from the Edge by James Hilton
(See bibliography)

Bloggers' corner

'This much I know about...how, as school leaders, we have to solve the recruitment crisis ourselves' by John Tomsett
Twitter handle: @johntomsett
(Link in bibliography)

TO DO LIST:

- ☐ Think about some staff who have left the school in the past one to two years.
- ☐ Are there any underlying reasons (apart from promotion) for them leaving?
- ☐ Are there any things that senior leaders could have done to create an environment that they didn't want to leave?
- ☐ Think about your current teams and the issues that some of them face.
- ☐ Can you do anything to resolve these issues?
- ☐ Read *Leading from the Edge* by James Hilton.
- ☐ Read 'This much I know about ... how, as school leaders, we have to solve the recruitment crisis ourselves' by John Tomsett.

19 Leaders as learners

Schools are buildings where learning takes place, but this certainly shouldn't be limited to just our students. In the ever-changing and dynamic educational landscape that we operate in, it is imperative that the leaders of our schools are constantly learning too. Every year there are new developments or changes to the way in which we need to operate. Whether it's a new Ofsted framework, government policy change, new research or educational thinking, or just a change of direction in your own school, there's always something to keep you on your toes. All of this does, however, require a mindset and a belief that you need to keep learning. Just because you've qualified as a teacher, maybe been on a senior leadership course or even passed your NPQH (National Professional Qualification for Headship), it doesn't mean anything if you believe that this makes you the finished article. These courses may prepare you to be effective in whatever stage of your career you are in, but without the attitude and ability to constantly adapt in today's educational world, you will only get so far.

The intrinsic motivation to constantly want to be the very best version of ourselves that we can be should be what drives us and our schools forward. A great quote from Dylan Wiliam sums this up perfectly: 'We can all be better, not because we need to be, but because we can be.' (2012) It's this type of attitude that should be adopted in every school boardroom across the world. Irrespective of how successful your school is, what results you have just achieved or the current Ofsted rating of the school, there are things that we can all do better. Our children deserve it too. Imagine going to a doctor and knowing that he or she isn't prepared to listen to new medical research and that they believe that the same procedures that were in place 20 or 30 years ago are still the most effective way to diagnose and deal with illness today. Would you be happy with this? As customers, clients, patients and parents, we expect that the people we are trusting with our money, health or children to be up to speed with new, cutting-edge developments in their field.

As teachers and leaders, we're also charged with being role models to our students. But how can we be role models to learners if we are not learners ourselves? Demonstrating to the wider school community that even the leaders of the school, the people who are supposed to be the most qualified and highly skilled, need to keep learning is the clearest message to everyone that life-long learning is paramount in any successful career. There should also be no shame in this, nor should your requirement to learn need to be hidden. An arrogance that you don't need to learn is a far worse trait to portray than an attitude that we all need to keep learning to be right at the top of our game.

Growth mindset

The growth mindset concept, developed by Carol Dweck (2017), has become a huge topic of conversation in schools across the world. The ability to get students to believe that their capacity to learn and succeed is not fixed by nature, but instead can be developed through effort and attitude, is being seen as a potential way to break down barriers to learning. But how much of this is being preached but not practised by teachers and leaders? I'm sure we've all experienced this type of 'Do what I say, don't do what I do' culture in some schools. If we can appreciate and acknowledge that a person's mindset has everything to do with how much they can learn and therefore how effective they can be at something, then why should this just be limited to the children we teach? Why shouldn't this apply just as much to the adults in the building as well as the students?

Growth mindset in practice

It seems quite absurd that lots of the practices that schools have tried to implement with their students over the years haven't been done with their staff first. Take for example professional development. Every teacher in your school knows that talking to a group of students for 30 minutes with no break and reading line by line off a PowerPoint presentation is classroom suicide. However, how many of us have sat through professional development sessions where that exact same thing happens to us? If we use this as an example, why then shouldn't we develop and practise a growth mindset approach to professional learning with our teachers, before we ask them to do the same with their students? Wouldn't this make the process far more in depth, with teachers actually believing in it, rather than just doing it because it's apparently the next big thing?

If we take this concept and adopt it as school leaders, then it will begin to eliminate the worry we all have when the inevitable changes to our working practices are required or forced upon us. Rather than be concerned about the fact you know nothing about what you've now been asked to do, or the fact that you feel you've never been that suited to or comfortable with a certain area of school leadership in the past, having a growth mindset lets you see this as a healthy challenge in your career – the type of challenge that motivates you to want to be better and one that will give you enormous satisfaction and pride once you master it. If we start to think more along the lines of 'how hard can it really be if someone else in a similar position to me is doing it?', then we might be able to start challenging ourselves to be a more well-rounded leader in all aspects of school leadership.

Failing schools with closed mindsets

Many failing or coasting schools also have a significant and urgent need for growth mindset amongst their leaders. It can be easy to see all of the problems surrounding your school as immovable barriers to progress. This defeatist attitude does nothing to move the school forward and instead just begins to permeate right through the school, with the whole workforce believing that factors outside of their control are holding their students back. Now I'm not saying for one minute that all failing or coasting schools have leaders with this attitude, or equally that some barriers are not immovable, but it's surprising what a fresh mindset can do to a seemingly impossible problem. One of the main issues with this is that leaders can get too close to the problems and too emotionally connected. Bringing in a fresh pair of eyes with no emotional or historical connection with the problem can be the best way to look at the problem differently. A new perspective, coupled with a growth mindset that this is just a challenge and not an immovable barrier, can bring about the seemingly impossible solution. Add to this the drive and energy that you don't get from someone who has been physically and emotionally bogged down by the problem for what seems like eternity, and it can make a huge difference in working towards a sustainable solution for school improvement.

A great way to practise this growth mindset concept in your everyday working life is to simply listen to other people. This is something that I picked up from a TED Talk by Celeste Headlee. In her 2015 talk, '10 ways to have a better conversation', she discussed how most people listen with the intent to reply, not with the intent to learn. Think about this from your own experiences of talking with people at school or at home. How many times have you stopped listening in a conversation because you are looking for a moment to interject with what you want to say? Celeste puts it beautifully that 'If that's all we're doing when we have a conversation, then it becomes more like two people shouting barely connected sentences at each other rather than a connected conversation.' Our listening skills are therefore absolutely key if we truly want to develop a growth mindset, because you never know when there's going to be an opportunity to learn something. Celeste says that we should all 'enter every conversation thinking that we have something to learn' and that 'if our mouth is open, then we're not learning' – simple and concise advice that we can all use to open our minds to the learning opportunities that exist all around us every day.

Networks

Once we have developed a growth mindset, or we are personally committed to opening our minds to the possibilities of learning from others and a desire to be better, we need to look for opportunities to do this. One of the most surprising things that I've experienced ever since I came into teaching is that teachers and leaders across the country are usually facing the same issues, but quite often feel that they have to develop a solution themselves in isolation from everyone else. I appreciate that, as previously mentioned in this book, all schools are set in different locations, contexts and settings, but the vast majority of issues and solutions can be transferable with a little bit of adaptation. Take for example the progress of white, male, pupil premium students. There's probably not a school leader in the land who can say that they've never had an issue with this group of students in their school.

By developing your own professional networks of likeminded leaders, both locally and nationally, you can then begin to tap into the thoughts, experience and advice of other leaders who are facing the exact same issues. Being able to sit down with a group of leaders and discuss how you've all tried to tackle a certain pressing issue in your schools, together with outlining the different approaches that have been both successful and unsuccessful, will make for a far better decision-making process when it comes to planning a solution to the problem. The beauty of these networks being both local and national means that you can gain a variety of ideas, thoughts and solutions from a range of different contexts. What works in one context might not work in another, but it may just be that the ability to see what is happening in a different area of the country is exactly what you need to open your mind to a significantly different approach to your problem.

Digital networks

With today's advances in digital technology, these networks don't even have to be face-to-face interactions that take up significant elements of people's time. Lots of outwardly thinking leaders now have online professional networks consisting of leaders from all over the world that they can call upon when they need some advice, support or guidance. Twitter has been a huge source of advice and inspiration for teachers and leaders in recent years and many professionals are now referencing networks like this as their number one source of professional development. This type of network is available as and when you need it and removes any barriers of cost, time and location. Just be careful to not just surround yourself with people who agree with you. Healthy challenge, or what Steve Munby calls 'group think', can thwart challenge because, with digital technology, it is now far too easy to block people you don't agree with and live in a bubble where you believe your own hype.

Visiting your networks

Even though talking, listening and networking are essential in developing a growth mindset approach to school improvement, you should not forget that seeing it and feeling it are extremely important. We can all talk for hours on end about what we do and how we do it, but until you physically see it in action, then you don't truly appreciate it. It's therefore always really good practice to try as much as you can to get out of you own school from time to time, to see other schools in action. This may be possible and easily set up through your professional networks as mentioned above. In all my time in education, in whatever role I've been in, I don't think I've ever not been able to come back with something from a school visit. It may just be a confirmation that you're doing the right thing, or it might be a conversation that leads onto another area of practice that you can take back and develop. The point is, though, that spending time in another setting, seeing how they do things differently to you, should never be underestimated. Far too often we get institutionalised in our schools by thinking that our way is the only way to do it. By establishing your networks and then using them to open your eyes to a different way of doing things, you can then begin to use your growth mindset to great benefit.

Supportive networks

Networks can also help with your own emotional strength when embarking on a school improvement journey. We need to remember that not all of the decisions we make will transform the school overnight. In fact, many of the solutions that we try to put in place might fail. However, if you are always operating in isolation, this can become quite disheartening and lead to an assumption that you are underperforming as a leader. The reality, though, is different. By being part of a network of supportive leaders, they will be able to share with you the failures and hurdles that they had to jump over, in order to get where they are. Understanding that all leaders have failures in some form can be comforting to hear, just as it is for your own students. Creating a fail-safe environment not only in our classrooms, but also for our school leaders, will enable us to be more adventurous and creative with our solutions, knowing that we have the support networks around us to discuss, analyse and evaluate our approaches before and after we implement them.

Chapter 19 takeaway

Teaching tip
Is there a growth mindset culture amongst your staff or your students? How can this be developed in your own professional life so that you can begin to learn from likeminded leaders locally, nationally and internationally?

Pass it on
Do you regularly talk to leaders in similar positions to the one you currently hold? How can you begin to either develop these networks or

use existing networks to look for solutions to some of the issues you are currently facing?

CPD book club recommendation
Perfect Teacher-Led CPD by Shaun Allison
(See bibliography)

Bloggers' corner
'Listen and learn. (Leading in stormy weather)' by Simon Smith
Twitter handle: @smithsmm
(Link in bibliography)

TO DO LIST:

- ☐ Develop your own local, national and international professional networks.
- ☐ Create a professional profile on Twitter/LinkedIn.
- ☐ Visit a variety of schools in different contexts to get a broader view of school improvement.
- ☐ Ask for advice and ideas from fellow colleagues when you have a significant problem to solve.
- ☐ Meet up regularly with likeminded leaders to discuss the topical issues that you are all facing in your schools.
- ☐ Enter into every conversation you have thinking you have something to learn.
- ☐ Read *Perfect Teacher-Led CPD* by Shaun Allison.
- ☐ Read 'Listen and learn. (Leading in stormy weather)' by Simon Smith.

Part 2

Train others

1 Leading professional development

Now that you've read Part 1 and you are a confident senior leader, it's time to pass on that knowledge to others. It's interesting to think about all of the training we get as classroom teachers during our career (and certainly through our initial teacher training), yet the same can't be said for leadership training. Most of the skills that we pick up are learned on the job, through trial and error. It is therefore essential that if we believe that leadership is the key to sustainable school improvement, we invest time into training our current and aspiring leaders to be world-class school leaders.

Having said this, one of the most overlooked areas of school improvement in many schools is the quality of professional development that a school offers its staff. As we discussed in Chapter 19, we are operating in a dynamic educational landscape, requiring us all to develop a growth mindset that ensures we are constantly learning and looking for new and improved ideas to raise the outcomes in our classrooms. As school leaders though, we can't just hope that this will happen. We need to create the environments in our schools and the opportunities for teachers to flourish in their own personal and professional development. Think of your teachers as cars. You wouldn't go to the petrol station and fill your tank up with water and expect it to run, would you? Or alternatively, leave it empty? Cars run on specific fuel to make the engine work and the car perform. This is the same for the teachers in our schools. How can you expect them to be performing at the very top of their game and be as good or better than other teachers across the country if the level of professional development they are receiving is poor or non-existent? Schools spend so much time, effort and money on intervening with students because, in lots of cases, the quality of teaching has not led to students hitting their targets. Yet quite remarkably, schools continue to do more of the same year on year, rather than investing more time, effort and money in quality professional development in a bid to halt this constant culture of intervention. Surely if we give more attention to the true development of staff as professionals, then we can begin to create a more sustainable model of school improvement, rather than relying on a sticky-plaster approach that just adds more stress and pressure to both staff and students.

Putting the 'professional' back into professional development

Continuous professional development (CPD) has been far from continuous or professional in many schools for too long. One-off professional development (PD) days that are mandatory for all staff have been historically scheduled in lots of schools at the start of the year and a generic whole-staff focus delivered to everyone, without choice. If you've experienced this, or if this model still exists in your own school, take a minute to think about the range of abilities, experience and skillsets amongst your staff. Can a one-size-fits-all session ever meet the needs of every one of your classroom staff?

- Is there ever an occasion where the whole of your staff requires the same development on a certain theme because they are all working at the same proficiency level?
- What happens after the PD day is finished?
- Does your school look to evaluate the training and run follow-up sessions to see how staff are progressing?
- Are staff just left to get on with it, without any further input until the next calendared PD in a few months' time?

Can this model really be called 'continuous' if it only happens a few times every year, or are the leaders in those schools just using their approach to professional development as another box to tick to say that they've covered a few of the latest buzz words in education? These leaders are then usually quite happy that when Ofsted walk through the door, they can say they have 'done' mindsets or resilience this year.

Reflect on your CPD

Take a few minutes to put down this chapter and reflect on your experience of your own professional development in the schools you have been employed in. Can you say that it has been 'professional'? Do you feel that the professional development that you've received over the years has made you into a significantly better teacher? What have been the highlights and lowlights of the professional development you have received? What are the main reasons for this? Once you've been able to reflect on your own experiences at the receiving end of professional development delivery, it is then vitally important to think about the quality of experiences that you or your team currently deliver. Is it any different to the experiences that you have just reflected on?

Irrespective of the quality that you believe you currently deliver, a leader with a growth mindset and a drive to always deliver improved standards will always be looking at how they can improve professional development. The best way that I have been able to do this is to focus on the word 'professional'. If we are working with professionals, then their training must be professional also. Ask yourself these questions about your current CPD programme:

- Could you sell it to other schools?
- Would people want to buy it?
- Would you be proud of it if you had to stand up at a national conference and speak about it?

If the answers to these questions are 'no', then it's probably telling you something about how 'professional' your professional development programme actually is.

Professional development should be done with people, not to people

Not only has professional development been delivered in one-size-fits-all sessions, but the delivery in lots of schools for lots of years has also been extremely poor. There isn't a single teacher worth their salt who would stand at the front of a class of students and read line by line from a PowerPoint presentation to their class for an hour and expect full engagement. However, some of those very same teachers deliver professional development to the whole of their staff in this very way! I've heard some people defend this method by suggesting that adults have a much higher attention span and can concentrate for longer periods of time, but if we know what engages and disengages our students, why wouldn't we employ the same strategies with our own staff when they are about to learn from us? We all know that we usually learn best when we are actively taking part in something, so why not model those very strategies that you want people to use as school leaders? You never know, it might just rub off on some leaders along the way.

Planning your CPD

Attention to detail is key when planning how you lead and deliver professional development. It's so easy to just throw together a PowerPoint presentation the night before you are delivering to a group of staff, but is that a professional approach to one of your potentially biggest school improvement strategies? Think about how many people are attending the session and then what the total hourly rate for all of those staff is going to be. Now think again about your preparation. Does it merit the amount of money that you are about to spend in staffing for that hour? Or do you need to start putting more time and energy into your planning?

Location

- Where will the session be held?
- Have you got enough room to accommodate everyone?
- Is your space the right size for the right amount of people?

It's important to think carefully about the space and make sure you use the right space for the right session. Don't think you always have to use the same space for all of your sessions.

Layout

- What type of floor plan do you want for your session? What is the most effective room layout for the activities you have planned?
- Do you want cabaret-style seating so that staff can communicate and collaborate in groups? Or do you want theatre-style seating where everyone is sat facing the front?
- Do you want faculty/subject staff sat together or mixed up to encourage cross-subject collaboration?
- Do you need to create a seating plan to strategically seat people to engineer effective collaboration?

Depending on the nature of your session, you may want different styles of seating. For example:

- Horse shoe: Seats curved like a horse shoe, all facing the front.
- Cabaret-style: Group tables that promote discussion and collaboration.
- Theatre-style: Rows of seats all facing the front (great if you want to maximise the amount of people in one venue).

Time

Delivering professional development sessions to staff after they have had a long day at work and taught five lessons might not be the smartest time to pick. Think about other times in the day that you might be able to use. Consider a breakfast session where staff can bring their breakfast or a cup of coffee along with them.

- Will a session at this time of the day tap into staff when they are fresh-minded?
- Will this also give them five lessons to try out their newly acquired skills straight after your session?

Innovative delivery methods

As previously discussed, the delivery method of professional development in many schools up and down the country leaves a lot to be desired. Rather than just delivering whole-staff sessions in the same way that you've always done it, why not start to think outside the box about different delivery methods that might engage your staff in a more professional approach?

The flipped approach

Using a flipped learning approach to deliver your professional development means that you can set your staff some pre-learning to do, before they attend the session. This might be in the form of watching a video or a screencast that you have created, or alternatively it might be something to read or think about. Either way, the main focus is on staff already coming to the session with the main ideas and already having had the time to digest them and reflect upon them. If this is done effectively, the sessions can then become more collaborative and discussion-based, rather than a traditional chalk-and-talk-style session.

The blended approach

The blended approach is similar to the flipped approach, in that some content is delivered outside of the session, usually as an extension. In this method, the presenter may direct the staff to further online resources to extend or broaden their knowledge of the topic after the session has finished. This way, staff can be independent in their further research after they have been given the initial input by the presenter. This can be a great way of getting people to master a topic in their own time, rather than just relying on the limited information you can give in one session.

The online approach

We all know that people learn at different speeds and in different ways, therefore bringing a whole group of staff together at any one time might not be that effective. Teachers will also have different needs at different times of the year and should not have to wait for the next PD day three months away to get the next instalment of their training and development. With the online method, you create a multitude of resources and videos covering as many areas of pedagogy as possible, so that staff can dip in and out of them at their leisure. This way, whenever a member of staff wants to learn, all they need to do is log in and access the specific modules that they require.

Think Pair Share

Think Pair Share is a great way to combine individual reflection and peer-discussion/reflection. Once you ask a question, get staff to think about the answer first on their own and then get them to pair up and discuss their thoughts. Once they have had sufficient time to engage in discussion, get pairs to report back to the group with their collaborative thoughts. This also helps with staff who might not be that confident in sharing their individual ideas and thoughts with the whole group.

Speed dating

Speed dating is a fantastic way of getting staff talking to staff and sharing ideas with people they would never normally communicate with. Simply set your hall or room up with lots of chairs facing each other and get people to randomly pair up. Set a timer for a short period of time (potentially three minutes) and get them to share an idea that they are each working on or that works in their classroom. When the time's up, facilitate a rotation so that everyone gets to meet someone new, before repeating the process.

Market stall

A market stall event is where each department, faculty or team sets up a stall of good practice that they are proud of. This may be a selection of books, schemes of learning, activities, resources, etc. The session is then an informal opportunity for all staff to visit all of the market stalls to see what other teams are doing. As long as one or two people are manning the stalls to answer questions, the rest of the team or department are free to wander the event. Get people to rotate between manning stalls and wandering the event so everyone gets a chance to see what's on offer.

Competitive professional development

Most of us like competition and when it's with our colleagues, it usually ends in fun. Therefore, think about ways in which you can make your professional development sessions have a competitive element. A great way to do this is to have a Christmas quiz. Collect a random supply of materials and items from a pound store and get the teams to come up with as many different ways that they can use them in a lesson as possible.

Compulsory vs. voluntary

It takes a brave leader to tell staff that attendance at professional development sessions is voluntary, but you have to ask yourself the question that if staff are only going because they have to, what does this say about the quality of your sessions? You can have the whole staff gathered for an after-school session, but if the majority of them don't want to be there, what impact are you going to get from it? Think about how you can introduce an element of fun to your professional development. If staff are enjoying it, they are more likely to remember it and therefore it will have more impact on them and their teaching over the longer term. If you put on high-quality sessions that staff really want to come to, you can then get staff attending because they want to, rather than simply because they are clocking their PD hours. You also shouldn't need to force people to attend professional development sessions if your appraisal system has rigour. If somebody has a development need, they should be attending the relevant sessions that you put on to address this. If they don't attend and they still have that development need the next time you appraise them, how can they expect to go through their pay progression?

However you decide to look at and reflect upon your own approach to delivering professional development, it needs to be professional and it needs to develop people. If you can create a culture of learning amongst your staff and get them excited about new strategies in the classroom, then you're already halfway there to creating a high-performing school with sustainability.

2 Training plans

This section includes a set of training plans to help you deliver high-quality training to aspiring senior leaders or senior leaders already in role. The training plans cover the key topics in Part 1 of the book and will support the ongoing development of leadership at all levels in your school.

The training plans

There are 17 training plans, with a total of 20 hours of training sessions.

The first 12 training plans are based on the content in Part 1 of the book:

1. What's the right role for you? (1 hour)
2. Developing your vision for school improvement (1 hour)
3. Developing a personal action plan (1 hour)
4. Understanding the context of a school (2 hours)
5. Building relationships (1 hour)
6. Running effective meetings (1 hour)
7. Leading difficult conversations (1 hour)
8. Successful staff recruitment (1 hour)
9. Thinking about staff wellbeing (1 hour)
10. Developing teachers into expert practitioners (1 hour)
11. Creating digital networks for professional learning (1 hour)
12. Holding people to account (1 hour)

As you've read Part 1 of the book, you will be familiar with the content and should feel confident running the sessions. However, each session is cross-referenced to the relevant chapter from Part 1, so as part of your preparation for the session you can always go back and read that chapter to refresh your memory. Training plans 13 to 17 are focused on delivering better professional development:

13. Planning and delivering an effective professional development day (2 hours)
14. Planning a conference and commercialising it (1 hour)
15. Planning a TeachMeet (1 hour)
16. Using a flipped learning approach for your professional development delivery (2 hours)
17. Creating video content for a flipped learning approach to professional development (1 hour)

As with the training plans from Part 1, all of the information and background reading you need to run these sessions can be found in Part 2, either in the form of a chapter or in a supplementary information sheet created for the session.

Overview

Each training plan includes an overview of the session:

- **Title**: The title of the session.
- **Aims**: What the attendees will get out of the session.
- **Duration**: The length of the session (this ranges between an hour and two hours).
- **Room layout**: Recommendation for how to set up the room.
- **Resources required and planning advice:** Everything you'll need for the session including the PowerPoints slides, the chapter reference and any extra planning considerations there might be for running the session.

Step-by-step guide

Each session includes a table detailing the following:

- **Phase:** The stage of the session, e.g. introduction, activity, plenary, next steps.
- **Timing:** How long this phase of the session should take.
- **Format:** The format the phase takes, e.g. presentation, demonstration, group work, individual reflection.
- **Content:** Instructions for how to run the phase.

PowerPoints and online resources

Each session includes a supporting PowerPoint presentation, which can be downloaded from the online resources at www.bloomsbury.com/cpd-library-senior-leadership and is fully editable so can be adapted to your needs and context. Supplementary information sheets and other additional resources can also be downloaded.

Planning the schedule of sessions

Depending on your context, you may decide to deliver these sessions weekly across a term, or in a more intensive leadership training day (or days) as part of a professional development day or residential course.

Who are the sessions for?

These training sessions could be delivered to a group of middle leaders in your school as part of a targeted leadership pathway, middle leaders from across neighbouring schools as part of a local authority aspiring leadership programme, or new or inexperienced senior leaders in your own school or beyond.

Before each session

Opening your session with the right feel can really make a difference. Make sure you:

- Arrive at the room at least 15 minutes before the session starts.
- Set up the room exactly as you want it.
- Have sufficient resources printed and ready.
- Put your PowerPoint or alternative presentation method on display, prior to delegates entering the room.
- Get the lighting as you want it, making sure it is suitable for viewing the presentation.

Greet people warmly as they arrive. Create a welcoming environment with a positive, upbeat yet calming presence. Consider having a thought-provoking statement or image on the projection screen as people enter to get them thinking right away.

Training plan 1

Overview

Title
What's the right role for you?

Aims
To give the participants the opportunity to think about the various senior leadership roles that exist in today's schools and to reflect on their own skillsets and interests in order to begin to identify the most suitable senior role for them.

Duration
1 hour

Room layout
Horse shoe

Resources required
- PowerPoint presentation: Training plan 1
- Part 1, Chapter 2: Senior leadership roles

Step-by-step guide to running the session

Phase	Timing	Format	Content
Introduction	15 mins	Presentation	• Introductory discussion about the three major areas of Ofsted that have senior leadership roles attached to them in most schools: 1. Quality of teaching and learning 2. Personal development, behaviour and welfare 3. Student outcomes • Brief discussion about a headteacher's role in pulling all of this together as part of the effectiveness of leadership and management that Ofsted also inspect.

Phase	Timing	Format	Content
Activity 1	15 mins	Think, Pair, Share	• Organise groups into pairs and ask them to discuss the following questions: o What is your current understanding and experience of the senior leadership positions that fall under these three areas? o What are the main roles that the people in these positions undertake on a weekly basis?
Activity 2	15 mins	Think, Pair, Share	• Pairs can stay the same or change depending on the quality of interactions. Questions to be discussed: o What key skills and characteristics do these people need in order to be successful in these positions? o Reflect on someone you have worked with in one of these roles (anonymously). What made them successful or unsuccessful?
Activity 3	10 mins	Individual reflection Pair discussion	• Encourage participants to now work on their own and think about the following: o List your current strengths and areas for further development. Which of the previously discussed roles do you suit best? • Discuss your reflections with a fellow participant. Compare and contrast your skillsets, experience and possible senior leadership roles.
Plenary and next steps	5 mins	Group discussion	• Recap the main points from the session. • Ask for individuals or pairs to feed back to the group on their reflections. • Summarise any key discussion points. • Identify next steps for individuals as they move towards being ready to apply for a senior leadership role. • Next steps tasks: o Talk to colleagues in your school who are in different senior leadership positions. Ask them about their roles, what they like and dislike about them. o Try to gain as much insight into the roles as you can from people who are currently doing them.

Training plan 2

Overview

Title

Developing your vision for school improvement

Aims

To give the participants the opportunity to think and reflect on their vision for school leadership and how it fits alongside their own morals and ethos for areas such as student behaviour, teaching and learning and student outcomes.

Duration

1 hour

Room layout

Horse shoe

Resources required

- PowerPoint presentation: Training plan 2
- Part 1, Chapter 9: Developing your vision for school improvement

Step-by-step guide to running the session

Phase	Timing	Format	Content
Introduction	10 mins	Presentation	• Introductory discussion about how it is essential to have a vision for school improvement as a senior leader. • Introduce the point that your own ethos for school improvement might not fit with the context of the school. An effective senior leader needs to blend their own personal ethos and vision with the needs of the school.

Phase	Timing	Format	Content

Activity 1	15 mins	Individual reflection	• Give participants seven minutes to consider the following questions individually:
			  o If you had a blank canvas, what would be your vision for personal development, behaviour and welfare in your school?
			  o What would student behaviour look like?
			  o How would you aim to get there?

		Think, Pair, Share	• Discuss your reflections with a fellow participant. Compare and contrast your thoughts.

Activity 2	15 mins	Individual reflection	• Ask participants to work individually again for seven minutes to consider:
			  o If you had a blank canvas, what would be your vision for the quality of teaching and learning in your school?
			  o What would outstanding teaching look like?
			  o How would you develop your current staff into expert practitioners?

		Think, Pair, Share	o Discuss your reflections with a fellow participant. Compare and contrast your thoughts.

Activity 3	15 mins	Individual reflection	• Ask participants to work individually once more for seven minutes to consider:
			  o If you had a blank canvas, what would be your vision for student outcomes and achievement in your school?
			  o How would you ensure that staff and student wellbeing is looked after, rather than your school just being an examination factory?

		Think, Pair, Share	• Discuss your reflections with a fellow participant. Compare and contrast your thoughts.

Plenary and next steps	5 mins	Group discussion	• Ask for individuals or pairs to feed back to the group on their reflections and where there were contrasting opinions.
			• Discuss how context might play a significant part in how your vision is formed.
			• Recap the main points from the session.
			• Identify next steps for individuals as they move towards being ready to apply for senior leadership roles.
			• Next steps tasks:
			  o Talking to the people on the ground in your new school can give you a fresh perspective on what you need to improve.
			  o Listen to their thoughts and look at ways in which you can resolve little issues quickly that will make a big difference to them.

Training plan 3

Overview

Title
Developing a personal action plan

Aims
To give the participants the opportunity to reflect on their own gaps that have been identified by their own 360 degree assessment and self-evaluation questionnaire, before beginning to structure their own action plan to address this.

Duration
1 hour

Room layout
Horse shoe

Resources required
- Participants should have completed the self-evaluation questionnaire (from Part 1, Chapter 1) or/and a 360 degree leadership assessment
- PowerPoint presentation: Training plan 3
- Part 1, Chapter 1: Are you ready? and Part 1, Chapter 3: Plugging your gaps

Step-by-step guide to running the session

Phase	Timing	Format	Content
Introduction	10 mins	Presentation	• Introductory discussion about the importance of understanding your own strengths and development points as a senior leader. • Brief discussion about all the different ways in which you can plug those gaps: o Existing colleagues and professional networks. o Visiting other schools. o External courses and books.

Phase	Timing	Format	Content

Activity 1	15 mins	Individual reflection and planning
		
		Think, Pair, Share
			• Give participants five minutes to reflect individually on the following:
			  o How can you use existing colleagues and professional networks to plug some of your gaps?
			• Then working in pairs ask them to:
			  o Begin to plan how and when this will happen.
			  o Are there any areas that your partner is using that you have not thought of?

Activity 2	15 mins	Individual reflection and planning
		
		Think, Pair, Share
			• Ask participants to work individually again for five minutes to consider:
			  o How can you use school visits to plug some of your gaps?
			  o Begin to plan how and when this will happen.
			• Then in pairs ask them to consider:
			  o Are there any areas that your partner is using that you have not thought of?

Activity 3	15 mins	Individual reflection and planning
		
		Think, Pair, Share
			• Working individually again for five minutes, ask participants to consider:
			  o How can you use external courses and books to plug some of your gaps?
			  o Begin to plan how and when this will happen.
			• Then in pairs ask them to consider:
			  o Are there any areas that your partner is using that you have not thought of?

Plenary and next steps	5 mins	Group discussion	• Ask for individuals or pairs to feed back on some of the methods they are going to use to plug some of their gaps.
			• Are there any type of gaps that are harder to plug than others?
			• Recap the main points from the session.
			• Identify next steps for individuals as they move towards being ready to apply for senior leadership roles.
			• Next steps tasks:
			  o You may find that there is another colleague in your school who is also looking to develop their own leadership skills.
			  o Why not work together to review each other's action plans and be a support for each other as you both move towards your respective professional goals?

Training plan 4

Overview

Title
Understanding the context of a school

Aims
To give the participants the opportunity to look in depth at a set of information about a fictional school and identify where the strengths and areas for school improvement are.

Duration
2 hours

Room layout
Cabaret-style with tables set out for group work

Resources required
- PowerPoint presentation: Training plan 4
- Blank action plan template (download from the online resources: Training Plan 4_Personal Leadership Action Plan)
- Fictional school information (school performance document, Ofsted report, School data)
- Part 1, Chapter 8: Understanding the school

Preparing for this session

In this session you are going to get the participants to prepare an action plan based on a set of fictional data about a school. Depending on your context, you may decide to use an old Ofsted report from your current school, or if you are training leaders from across a local area, you might want to create a fictional document, made up from multiple inspection reports from different schools.

Step-by-step guide to running the session

Phase	Timing	Format	Content

Introduction	10 mins	Presentation	• Introductory discussion about the various pieces of information that can enable you to understand a school, its context, performance and where it needs to improve. They are:
			  o Ofsted report.
			  o School performance document or FFT Aspire data.
			  o In-school data, for example, progress and attainment data and attendance and exclusion figures.

Activity 1	30 mins	Small group task (three to four per group)	• Using the latest Ofsted report on the school, identify three priorities for school improvement. • Create a plan for your first few months in a specific senior leadership role at the school in the template provided.
Activity 2	30 mins	Small group task (three to four per group)	• Using the latest school performance document or FFT Aspire, identify the priorities for school improvement. • Add your intended interventions to your action plan template.
Activity 3	30 mins	Small group task (three to four per group)	• Using the latest in-school data, identify the priorities for school improvement. • Add your intended interventions to your action plan.
Activity 4	15 mins	Group discussion	• Group discussion and sharing of thoughts on the identified areas of improvement required at the school.

Plenary and next steps	5 mins	Group discussion	• Recap the main points from the session.
			• Identify next steps and personal gaps in experience of skillsets (when analysing school information data) as they move towards being ready to apply for senior leadership roles.
			• Next steps tasks:
			  o Talk to your new colleagues. They will hold lots of interesting information that you'll not find in a school performance document.
			  o Their views and interpretations of the data and the school context might give you a more valuable viewpoint to consider.

Training plan 5

Overview

Title
Building relationships

Aims
To give the participants the opportunity to think about all the professional relationships that need to be built and developed, both in school and in the local community, in order to be a successful and effective school leader.

Duration
1 hour

Room layout
Horse shoe

Resources required
- PowerPoint presentation: Training plan 5
- Part 1, Chapter 10: Building professional relationships and Part 1, Chapter 11: Building community relationships

Step-by-step guide to running the session

Phase	Timing	Format	Content

Introduction	10 mins	Presentation	• Introductory discussion about how it is essential to build positive relationships as quickly as you can in your new role as a senior leader.
			• Introduce the different groups of people that are important to build relationships with, both in school and in the local community:
			  o In-school: teachers, support staff, fellow senior leaders and governors.
			  o Community groups: parents, residents, businesses, local media, religious groups.

Phase	Timing	Format	Content

Activity 1	15 mins	Individual reflection	• Give participants seven minutes to work individually to think about why it is important to develop strong positive relationships with the different groups of people in your school.
			  o How can you begin to develop these relationships?
			  o What would you do?

		Think, Pair, Share	• Discuss your reflections with a fellow participant. • Compare and contrast your thoughts.

Activity 2	15 mins	Individual reflection	• Ask participants to work individually again for seven minutes to think about why it is important to develop strong positive relationships with the different groups of people in the local community.
			  o How can you begin to develop these relationships?
			  o What would you do?

		Think, Pair, Share	• Discuss your reflections with a fellow participant. • Compare and contrast your thoughts.
Activity 3	15 mins	Individual reflection	• For a final seven minutes, ask individuals to consider: o As a new senior leader, how could you make some quick wins with any of the groups that we have identified?
		Think, Pair, Share	• Discuss your reflections with a fellow participant. • Compare and contrast your thoughts.
Plenary and next steps	5 mins	Group discussion	• Ask for individuals or pairs to feed back to the group on their reflections. • Recap the main points from the session. • Identify next steps for individuals as they move towards being ready to apply for senior leadership roles. • Next steps tasks: o Take the time to talk to cleaners, office staff, teachers and governors. All of these people play a significant part in your school improvement plans, so they should all be treated with equal measures of respect.

Training plan 6

Overview

Title
Running effective meetings

Aims
To give the participants the opportunity to reflect on how to run effective meetings, whilst giving them the opportunity to plan and practise their skills.

Duration
1 hour

Room layout
Cabaret-style with tables set out for group work

Resources required
- PowerPoint presentation: Training plan 6
- Part 1, Chapter 13: Effective meetings

Step-by-step guide to running the session

Phase	Timing	Format	Content

Introduction	10 mins	Presentation	• Introductory discussion about how the face-to-face time we have with colleagues is so precious that our meetings need to be productive and efficient.
			• Discussion around the cost of team meetings, given how much money is in the room from a human resources perspective, giving the examples:
			  o What's the hourly rate of everyone sat in your meeting?
			  o What is the total human resource cost of that meeting?

Phase	Timing	Format	Content
Activity 1	15 mins	Group task (groups of three or four)	• Groups are given a scenario from which they need to plan a team meeting: o Your faculty has just been through an internal review. Lessons were poor, some books were not marked and student behaviour was not good. There are two weeks to go before the Christmas holidays and staff are tired. • Groups need to decide on the format, time, location and agenda.

Activity 2	15 mins	Role play	• Each member of the group needs to lead a separate part of the meeting they have just planned.
			• Different scenarios should be planned for so that leaders can demonstrate how they would ensure a productive meeting takes place. For example:
			  o If a meeting gets heated.
			  o If team members disagree with the leader.
			  o If people become upset.

Activity 3	10 mins	Presentation	• How can you use a flipped learning approach to flip your team meetings? • If team members had access to key information and documents prior to the meeting (that were to be discussed in the meeting), would it make meetings more streamlined and efficient?
Plenary and next steps	10 mins	Group discussion	• Ask for groups to feed back on techniques and strategies that were effective in their role play scenarios. • Recap the main points from the session. • Identify next steps for individuals as they move towards being ready to apply for senior leadership roles. • Next steps tasks: o Take the time to speak to your colleagues about how meetings have been run previously. You'll be able to pick up whether there is any resentment for meetings and how effectively (or not) they have been run.

Training plan 7

Overview

Title
Leading difficult conversations

Aims
To give the participants the opportunity to reflect on how to successfully conduct difficult conversations, whilst giving them the opportunity to plan and practise their skills.

Duration
1 hour

Room layout
Cabaret-style with tables set out for group work

Resources required
- PowerPoint presentation: Training plan 7
- Part 1, Chapter 14: Difficult conversations

Step-by-step guide to running the session

Phase	Timing	Format	Content
Introduction	10 mins	Presentation	• Introductory discussion about how difficult conversations are an essential part of leadership when you are holding people to account.
		Group discussion	• In groups, ask participants to discuss why some difficult conversations have gone wrong in the past (both delivering these and being on the receiving end of these experiences).

Phase	Timing	Format	Content

Activity 1	5 mins	Individual planning for a difficult conversation	• Individuals choose a scenario to plan a difficult conversation around from the following options:
			  o One of your team is getting into school only a couple of minutes before lessons begin.
			  o You notice inappropriate comments on a social media account belonging to one of your team.
			  o A male member of your team has started to dress very casually for work and not wear a tie.
			  o A member of your team has started missing their break time duty, claiming they are too busy with marking.
			  o There is a sudden hike in behaviour points from a well-respected and experienced member of your team.
			  o You discover that a member of your team has not been marking any of their books for the past six weeks.
			• Individually, participants should plan:
			  o How the conversation will take place.
			  o Where and when it will take place.
			  o What the intended outcomes will be.

Activity 2	30 mins	Role play	• Individuals then pair up with another leader to practise their difficult conversations.
			  o Each conversation should take five minutes (ten minutes per pair) before swapping and having the conversation with another partner. Swap with three different partners.
			  o Participants on the receiving end of the conversation need to be in role and be as difficult as possible.

Activity 3	10 mins	Group discussion	• What tactics did people use to make the conversation more difficult for you to lead? • How did you manage this effectively? • What strategies did you use to keep the conversation on track?

Plenary and next steps	5 mins	Group discussion	• Recap the main points from the session.
			• Identify next steps for individuals as they move towards being ready to apply for senior leadership roles.
			• Next steps tasks:
			  o Although we don't want to go looking for conflict, make sure that you don't duck your next opportunity to have a difficult conversation.
			  o Be confident and tackle the issue with authority.

Training plan 8

Overview

Title
Successful staff recruitment

Aims
To give the participants the opportunity to reflect on their own recruitment strategies and how can they be more effective and successful when advertising and marketing vacancies.

Duration
1 hour

Room layout
Cabaret-style with tables set out for group work

Resources required
- PowerPoint presentation: Training plan 8
- Part 1, Chapter 17: Recruitment of high-quality staff

Step-by-step guide to running the session

Phase	Timing	Format	Content
Introduction	10 mins	Presentation	• Introductory discussion about how recruiting high-quality staff is so important.
		Group discussion	• Discussion about the issues and barriers schools face when trying to recruit teaching staff.

Phase	Timing	Format	Content

Activity 1	15 mins	Group task (groups of three or four)	• Groups are given a scenario from which they need to plan a recruitment strategy:
			  o You are looking for a head of maths.
			  o You are a 'requires improvement' school.
			  o Results were below the national average last year.
			  o The school is a new building.
			  o You are located in a large city.
			  o A new headteacher started at the school last term.
			• Groups need to decide on how and where they will advertise the vacancy.

Activity 2	15 mins	Group task (groups of three or four)	• Groups need to decide what to include in the pack that will be sent out to all interested candidates. • What will make your pack stand out from the rest?
Activity 3	15 mins	Group task (groups of three or four)	• Groups need to decide on the interview format. • How can you ensure that you test the candidates in as many areas as you deem are important in a one-day interview?

Plenary and next steps	5 mins	Group discussion	• Ask for groups to feed back on any innovative methods that they came up with to ensure they were able to recruit the very best teachers.
			• Recap the main points from the session.
			• Identify next steps for individuals as they move towards being ready to apply for senior leadership roles.
			• Next steps tasks:
			  o Talk to people about their experiences of being on the other side of the process.
			  o Where do they look for job adverts? What would entice them to apply for another job at another school?

Training plan 9

Overview

Title
Thinking about staff wellbeing

Aims
To give the participants the opportunity to reflect on staff wellbeing in their school and develop successful strategies that lead to increased staff wellbeing.

Duration
1 hour

Room layout
Cabaret-style with tables set out for group work

Resources required
- PowerPoint presentation: Training plan 9
- Part 1, Chapter 18: Retention, development and wellbeing

Step-by-step guide to running the session

Phase	Timing	Format	Content
Introduction	10 mins	Presentation	• Introductory discussion about how the wellbeing of staff is so important if you want to have a sustainable school improvement strategy.
		Group discussion	• Discussion about the biggest issues in school today in relation to staff wellbeing.

Phase	Timing	Format	Content

Activity 1	15 mins	Group task (groups of three or four)	• Groups are given a scenario from which they need to plan a staff wellbeing strategy.
			  o You are a 'requires improvement' school.
			  o Results were well below the national average last year.
			  o There is a high turnover of staff.
			  o Quite a few high-performing staff have left to work in the neighbouring school.
			  o There are three members of staff currently signed off with stress.
			• Groups need to decide on how they can promote physical wellbeing amongst their staff.

Activity 2	15 mins	Group task (groups of three or four)	• Groups need to decide how to promote practical wellbeing amongst their staff. • What practical strategies can you share with staff to help with their personal organisation?
Activity 3	15 mins	Group task (groups of three or four)	• Groups need to decide how to promote digital wellbeing amongst their staff. • How can you ensure that your staff have 'down time' away from school and do not feel that they are constantly bombarded by digital communication on evenings and weekends?

Plenary and next steps	5 mins	Group discussion	• Ask for groups to feed back on any innovative methods that they came up with to ensure that staff wellbeing is at the forefront of people's minds.
			• Recap the main points from the session.
			• Identify next steps for individuals as they move towards being ready to apply for senior leadership roles.
			• Next steps tasks:
			  o When was the last time you asked your team what they value at school and what would make their jobs even more enjoyable or satisfying?
			  o By opening up this dialogue, you may be able to create an even more productive and satisfying environment at school.

Training plan 10

Overview

Title
Developing teachers into expert practitioners

Aims
To give the participants the opportunity to reflect on their approach to professional development and whether it is truly developing staff into expert practitioners.

Duration
1 hour

Room layout
Cabaret-style with tables set out for group work

Resources required
- PowerPoint presentation: Training plan 10
- Part 2, Chapter 1: Leading professional development

Step-by-step guide to running the session

Phase	Timing	Format	Content
Introduction	10 mins	Presentation	• Introductory discussion about how high-quality professional development is essential if you want your teachers to be expert practitioners.
		Group discussion	• Discussion and reflection on people's experiences of professional development and whether it's professional or has developed them.
Activity 1	15 mins	Group task (groups of three or four)	• How can you ensure that professional development meets the needs of all the staff in your school? • How can you move away from a one-size-fits-all approach?
		Group discussion	• Feed back to group with innovative ideas.

Phase	Timing	Format	Content
Activity 2	15 mins	Group task (groups of three or four) Group discussion	• What strategies can you put in place to aid the retention of staff, through a highly respected and sought-after professional development programme? • How does your professional development programme consider succession planning for your middle and senior leadership roles? • Feed back to group with innovative ideas.
Activity 3	15 mins	Group task (groups of three or four) Group discussion	• How are you going to evaluate how effective your professional development programme is? • What key performance indicators or evidence are you going to use to determine this? • Feed back to group with innovative ideas.
Plenary and next steps	5 mins	Group discussion	• Recap the main points from the session. • Identify next steps for individuals as they move towards being ready to apply for senior leadership roles. • Next steps tasks: o Think about how 'professional' your professional development offer is. Speak to your colleagues to get their views. o Are you doing things the same way you've always done them? How innovative and effective is it?

Training plan 11

Overview

Title
Creating digital networks for professional learning

Aims
To give the participants the opportunity to look at using Twitter as a professional learning network for their own development.

Duration
1 hour

Room layout
Horse shoe

Resources required
- PowerPoint presentation: Training plan 11
- Part 1, Chapter 19: Leaders as learners
- Training plan 11 supplementary information sheet: Using Twitter as a professional learning network (see page 189 and can be downloaded as a handout for participants)
- Trainer will need to have their own Twitter account ready to demonstrate
- Delegates to have own devices (or laptops) ready to log in to Twitter

Step-by-step guide to running the session

Phase	Timing	Format	Content
Introduction	10 mins	Presentation	• Introductory discussion about how it is essential for us all to keep learning as leaders.
		Group discussion	• Whole-group discussion about growth mindset and what it means to us as leaders. • How can leaders adopt a growth mindset as well as the students we teach?

Phase	Timing	Format	Content
Activity 1	15 mins	Presentation	• Introduction to using Twitter as a professional learning network. • Look at the differences when using social media professionally, as opposed to only personally.
		Hands-on, with staff using personal devices	• How to set up your account and bio so that it reflects a professional approach.
Activity 2	15 mins	Presentation and demonstration on the benefits of having a professional learning network	• How to make the most out of a professional learning network. • Who to follow? What to look for? • How can it be used to develop your knowledge and keep you up to date with educational thinking?
Activity 3	15 mins	Presentation and demonstration	• What are hashtags? • How do they work? • Why would I want to use one when I tweet? • Why would I want to search for one?
Plenary and next steps	5 mins	Group discussion	• How can we keep ourselves safe and professional when posting about education? • Recap the main points from the session. • Identify next steps for individuals as they move towards being ready to apply for senior leadership roles • Next steps tasks: o How can you begin to develop professional networks, or use existing networks to look for solutions to some of the issues you are currently facing?

Using Twitter as a professional learning network

Why use Twitter?

Twitter is the most diverse professional development network there is. It is filled with teachers and leaders from all over the world talking about education. Lots of teachers now say it has been their best source of professional development over the past few years.

What are the differences between using it personally and professionally?

When using a social network like Twitter professionally, it's important to remember that it's not the place to be posting pictures of what you're having for dinner or pictures of you on nights out. Make sure you use other networks (or a separate profile) for this. Keep it professional and about education.

How do you set up your account and biography for professional use?

Use a professional picture (possibly your work picture from your ID badge) and then construct your profile around the role you do and the experience or interest you have in education. This way, people will be able to know a little more about you and feel they can connect with you if they have similar interests and experience.

How do you make the most out of a professional learning network?

Follow lots of interesting teachers and leaders from around the world, read their tweets and their blogs and feel free to interact with them and join in the global conversation about education. The advice you can get from teachers and leaders across the globe is like nothing you'd ever be able to replicate in your own staffroom.

What are hashtags? Why use them?

Hashtags let people tag an article with a certain word, meaning that you can click on that hashtag and be taken to all the tweets that have been tagged with that specific hashtag. This is great when speaking to people about a certain topic, especially if lots of people around the world are talking about the same thing. By simply clicking on the hashtag, you're instantly transported into the global conversation about that topic.

How can you keep yourself safe when tweeting about education?

Simple rule of thumb... only post something that you wouldn't mind your headteacher or a parent of one of your students reading. If you follow this rule, you usually can't go wrong.

Where can I get more information?

Ross Morrison McGill (@TeacherToolkit on Twitter) has written a great article on how to get started and why all teachers should be using Twitter: '10 tips for tweeting teachers' which you can find here: www.teachertoolkit. co.uk/2014/08/01/10-tips-for-tweeting-teachers-by-teachertoolkit.

Training plan 12

Overview

Title
Holding people to account

Aims
To give the participants the opportunity to reflect on and practise holding people to account for their roles and responsibilities.

Duration
1 hour

Room layout
Cabaret-style with tables set out for group work

Resources required
- PowerPoint presentation: Training plan 12
- Part 1, Chapter 14: Difficult conversations and Part 1, Chapter 15: Holding people to account

Step-by-step guide to running the session

Phase	Timing	Format	Content
Introduction	10 mins	Presentation	• Introductory discussion about how it is essential for leaders to be able to effectively hold people to account. • Discussion about what 'accountability at all levels' means to people.

Phase	Timing	Format	Content

Activity 1	5 mins	Individual planning for a conversation where you need to hold someone to account	• Individuals choose a scenario to plan an accountability conversation around, from the following examples:
			  o In a recent work scrutiny you find that a member of staff has not marked their books at all this term.
			  o A colleague that you line manage has not made any progress on their action plan since the last time you met them, even though they'd told you they had.
			  o A member of staff is repeatedly not submitting their classroom registers.
			  o As the senior lead link to a faculty, you meet with the faculty leader about their recent poor examination results.
			  o As the senior leader responsible for attendance, you meet with the Head of Year 11 due to poor attendance in the year group.
			• What actions are required? How and by when?

Activity 2	30 mins	Role play	• Individuals pair up with another leader to practise their accountability conversations. • Conversations should take five minutes each before swapping (ten minutes per pair). Swap with three different partners. • Participants on the receiving end of the accountability conversation need to be in role and try to be as evasive as possible in order to escape accountability.
Activity 3	10 mins	Group discussion	• What tactics did people use to make the accountability conversation more difficult for you to pin them down to actions and timelines? • How did you manage this effectively? What strategies did you use to ensure that the member of staff was very clear about your expectations?

Plenary and next steps	5 mins	Group discussion	• Recap the main points from the session.
			• Identify next steps for individuals as they move towards being ready to apply for senior leadership roles.
			• Next steps tasks:
			  o Model accountability practices to the staff whom you lead and talk to them about the importance of it as a key school improvement strategy.
			  o Tell them that you expect them to do the same with the people they lead.

Training plan 13

Overview

Title
Planning and delivering an effective professional development day

Aims
To give the participants the opportunity to reflect on and plan how to deliver an effective professional development day for the whole staff in your school.

Duration
2 hours

Room layout
Cabaret-style with tables set out for group work

Resources required
- PowerPoint presentation: Training plan 13
- Part 2, Chapter 1: Leading professional development
- All participants need to bring with them a range of resources from their faculty or school that demonstrates their approach to marking and feedback.

Step-by-step guide to running the session

Phase	Timing	Format	Content
Introduction	10 mins	Presentation	• Introductory discussion about professional development days and their purpose.
		Reflection and discussion	• Reflect on the last couple of PD days you've been involved in: o How effective have they been? o Why was this?

Phase	Timing	Format	Content
Activity 1	10 mins	Presentation and discussion	• How can you make the day engaging and inspirational? • What different and innovative styles of delivery can you use to engage your staff? • Think about the different methods you have used or been part of previously. • Which ones have been the most effective in engaging staff?
Activity 2	20 mins	Role play	• Participants take part in a speed-dating-style session. This will demonstrate how this style of delivery could be used as part of the PD day. • Participants move from one person to another every four minutes. • Each person gets two minutes to talk about the one thing that's made the biggest difference to their teaching over the past two years.
Activity 3	20 mins	Role play	• Participants take part in a market-stall-style session. This will demonstrate how this style of delivery could be used as part of the PD day. • Participants are split into two groups. Group A set up their marking and feedback examples and resources on their table (these resources were listed in the 'resources required' section). Group B get ten minutes to wander around the room to stop and ask questions at each stall. • After ten minutes, groups switch over and repeat the exercise.
Activity 4	10 mins	Group discussion	• Review and evaluation of the previous two activities. • Were they engaging? • Are they an effective alternative to the traditional approach to PD days? • Would they engage your staff?
Activity 5	15 mins	Think, Pair, Share	• How can you make the PD day fun? • Are there any ways that you can add elements of competition into the day? • Will this lead to more engagement, especially if it's the first day back after a holiday?

Phase	Timing	Format	Content
Activity 6	15 mins	Think, Pair, Share	• What is the most effective room layout for the activities that you might be planning? o Theatre-style, group tables, horse shoe, etc. • Should you have faculty/subject staff seated together, or do you want to mix them up? Is this the same for all your activities? • Do you need a seating plan to strategically seat people together or away from each other?
Activity 7	15 mins	Individual task	• Plan a two-hour PD day that has to focus on the quality of feedback that students receive. • Think about how you can make it as engaging and effective as possible. • The PD day is the first day back in January.

Plenary and next steps	5 mins	Group discussion	• Ask for individuals to feed back to the group on any reflections they might have.
			• Recap the main points from the session.
			• Identify next steps for individuals or schools as they plan for their next PD day.
			• Next steps tasks:
			  o Talk to staff about their experiences of staff PD days.
			  o What do they like? What do they remember? What formats do they feel engage them more in their professional learning?

Training plan 14

Overview

Title

Planning a conference and commercialising it

Aims

To give the participants the opportunity to reflect on and plan how to deliver an effective conference for teachers from across the region.

Duration

1 hour

Room layout

Cabaret-style with tables set out for group work

Resources required

- PowerPoint presentation: Training plan 14
- Training plan 14 supplementary information sheet: Planning a conference and commercialising it (see page 198 and can be downloaded as a handout for participants)

Step-by-step guide to running the session

Phase	Timing	Format	Content
Introduction	10 mins	Presentation	• Introductory discussion about how you can start to commercialise your professional development activities by bringing in guest speakers and selling tickets to other schools.
Activity 1	15 mins	Group task (groups of three or four) Group discussion	• How can you bring a top-class speaker into your school? Where would you find one? • What would they cost? • How can you ensure that a visiting speaker is going to be good value for money? • Feed back to group with innovative ideas.

Phase	Timing	Format	Content
Activity 2	15 mins	Group task (groups of three or four)	• How would you form your pricing strategy for the tickets you sell? • Do you just want to break even? Or do you want to make a profit? • Are there any sponsorship opportunities to reduce your costs? • Will you provide refreshments to delegates? Will there be a charge?
		Group discussion	• Feed back to group with innovative ideas.
Activity 3	15 mins	Group task (groups of three or four)	• How are you going to promote your event so that it at least breaks even? • Where are the best places to advertise? • Will your advertising impact on your pricing strategy?
		Group discussion	• Feed back to group with innovative ideas.

Plenary and next steps	5 mins	Group discussion	• Recap the main points from the session.
			• Identify next steps for individuals as they think about planning a commercially viable conference.
			• Next steps tasks:
			  o Attend a professional learning conference and evaluate it.
			  o Could you organise something similar on a local level?

Planning a conference and commercialising it

Why should you start to commercialise your professional development activities?

Bringing in a top-class speaker to speak to your staff may seem unrealistic due to cost. However, why not sell tickets to other local schools so that you can cover some of the cost and make it a realistic proposition?

How can you bring a top-class speaker to your school? Where do you find them?

Use your professional learning network (if you have one), or contact a professional development company that advertises local and national courses. They will probably be happy to run an event at your school, but it will come at a cost.

What will a speaker typically cost?

Speakers can cost anywhere from approximately £500 upwards depending on the quality.

How can you ensure they will be value for money?

Do your homework on them. Ask other schools who've previously booked them. Were they good? Did they justify their fee? Have they had an impact on the school since the session?

How will you form your pricing strategy?

It all depends if you are just happy to break even or if you are looking to make a profit. Like with any pricing strategy, the cheaper you make the tickets, the more you'll probably sell. Think about what your minimum number of sales needs to be to break even.

What sponsorship opportunities are there?

Education companies across the country are always looking to sponsor events because they have got a captive audience for their products. You might find that a company is prepared to give you between £300 and £500 for just being able to put a stand up in your venue, or put flyers on the table. You might want to ask for a little more if they get the chance to speak as well.

Should you provide refreshments?

Refreshments are always something that people like, especially if they are there all day (this would be a must), or if they have just come from a full day of teaching. However, don't forget about the price of these when you're thinking about your pricing strategy.

How do you promote and advertise your event?

Market your event wherever you know there is an education audience. The best way seems to be through places like Twitter and Facebook, alongside the traditional email route.

Training plan 15

Overview

Title
Planning a TeachMeet

Aims
To give the participants the opportunity to reflect on and plan how to deliver an effective TeachMeet for teachers from across the region.

Duration
1 hour

Room layout
Cabaret-style with tables set out for group work

Resources required
- PowerPoint presentation: Training plan 15
- Training plan 15 supplementary information sheet: Planning a TeachMeet (see page 202 and can be downloaded as a handout for participants)

Step-by-step guide to running the session

Phase	Timing	Format	Content
Introduction	10 mins	Presentation Group discussion	• Introductory discussion about what a TeachMeet is. • Why are TeachMeets popular? • Has anyone been to a TeachMeet? What made it successful or unsuccessful?

Phase	Timing	Format	Content
Activity 1	15 mins	Group task (groups of three or four)	• Do you want to have a theme for your TeachMeet? • What are the advantages and disadvantages of having a keynote speaker at your TeachMeet? • Have you been to a TeachMeet where there has been a keynote speaker? Does this add to or detract from the event? • Will there be a cost to having a keynote speaker?
		Group discussion	• Feed back to group with innovative ideas.
Activity 2	15 mins	Group task (groups of three or four)	• How can you use sponsors to help with some of the running costs? • Do you want to have prizes for members of the audience or some of the speakers? Will this entice people to attend? • How can you ensure that the sponsors do not take over the event from a commercial perspective?
		Group discussion	• Feed back to group with innovative ideas.
Activity 3	15 mins	Group task (groups of three or four)	• Think about the logistics of the event. • How long can people speak for? • How many speaker slots are you prepared to have? • How can you ensure that speakers are teachers and not just companies promoting their products? • Will delegates receive refreshments? • How can you make the event as fun and as memorable as possible?
		Group discussion	• Feed back to group with innovative ideas.
Plenary and next steps	5 mins	Group discussion	• Recap the main points from the session. • Identify next steps for individuals as they think about planning a TeachMeet. • Next steps tasks: o Attend a TeachMeet and evaluate its effectiveness.

Planning a TeachMeet

What is a TeachMeet?

A TeachMeet is a gathering of teachers coming together to share ideas on stage and learn from one another. Typically, teachers sign up to either present an idea on stage or just sit in the audience. Presentations are normally timed to only a few minutes, enabling lots of presentations in one evening.

Should you have a theme for your TeachMeet?

There is no rule for this. You might decide to have a theme of something like digital technology, but on the other hand you might just want to leave it open so that there is a diverse range of strategies presented.

Should you have a keynote speaker?

Again, this is purely down to preference. Having a keynote speaker sometimes adds more excitement to the event and draws in more people, but other times it takes the focus away from the teachers who are there to present what works in their classroom.

How can you use sponsors to help with running costs?

Education companies across the country are always looking to sponsor events because they have got a captive audience for their products. You might find that a company is prepared to give you between £300 and £500 for just being able to put a stand up in your venue, or put flyers on the table. Companies also like sponsoring prizes on the evening. This can be great to create excitement.

How can you ensure your event doesn't become to commercialised by the influence of sponsors?

A general rule of thumb for TeachMeets is that the only people presenting should be teachers, not companies trying to sell their products. Most people appreciate that there needs to be some way of generating income to cover costs, so flyers on tables and a stand at the back of the hall are acceptable.

How can you market the event?

Market your event wherever you know there is an education audience. The best way seems to be through places like Twitter and Facebook, alongside the traditional email route.

How should I plan the event?

Think about the structure of the event. How many presentation slots do you want? How long do you want each slot to be? Are you going to introduce each speaker? How are they going to present? Do you want their presentations sent through beforehand?

Training plan 16

Overview

Title

Using a flipped learning approach for your professional development delivery

Aims

To give the participants the opportunity to reflect on and plan how to use a flipped learning approach in the delivery of their professional development programmes at school.

Duration

2 hours

Room layout

Cabaret-style with tables set out for group work

Resources required

- PowerPoint presentation: Training plan 16
- Part 2, Chapter 1: Leading professional development

Step-by-step guide to running the session

Phase	Timing	Format	Content
Introduction	15 mins	Presentation Reflection and discussion	• Introductory discussion about what flipped learning is. • Has anyone used a flipped learning approach in their classrooms? What makes it effective?

Phase	Timing	Format	Content

Activity 1	15 mins	Presentation followed by group discussion (in groups of three or four)	• Discussion around the logistics of flipped learning prior to the session:
			  o What takes place prior to the session?
			  o What is the best way to ensure that this happens and that participants complete their pre-session learning?
			  o Why do you want students to have this information before they arrive at the session?

Activity 2	15 mins	Presentation followed by group discussion (in groups of three or four)	• Discussion around the logistics of flipped learning in the session itself:
			  o What takes place in the session?
			  o How can you maximise your face-to-face time with your participants?
			  o What can the participants now do because they have already come with the knowledge gained from their pre-session learning?
			  o How will your delivery style now be different?

Activity 3	15 mins	Group discussion (in groups of three or four)	• How can this approach be applied to professional development sessions • Will it work for all the topics that you deliver throughout the year? • What are the pros and cons of using this approach with adults? • Feed back to group with innovative ideas.
Activity 4	15 mins	Group discussion (in groups of three or four)	• What type of mediums can you use for pre-session learning with your staff? • Might you use different mediums for different topics? • Might you use different mediums for different groups of staff? • Feed back to group with innovative ideas.

Phase	Timing	Format	Content
Activity 5	15 mins	Group discussion (in groups of three or four)	• How can you ensure that staff complete their pre-session learning? • What happens if they don't complete their pre-session learning? • How can you motivate staff to want to learn in this way? • Feed back to group with innovative ideas.
Activity 6	25 mins	Individual planning	• Plan an upcoming professional development session in a flipped learning style. • What will staff do prior to the session. How will this happen? • What will staff do in the session?

Plenary and next steps	5 mins	Group discussion	• Ask for individuals to feed back to the group on any reflections they might have from their individual planning.
			• Recap the main points from the session.
			• Identify next steps for individuals or schools as they plan to use a flipped learning approach to professional development.
			• Next steps tasks:
			  o Further reading on flipped learning and the benefits of using such an approach.
			  o Speak to staff in your school. Are any of them using a flipped approach with their students? If so, go and see it in action and then think about how this might work with adults.

Training plan 17

Overview

Title
Creating video content for a flipped learning approach to professional development

Aims
To give the participants the opportunity to think about and plan how they would create video content as part of the pre-session learning for a professional development session using a flipped learning approach.

Duration
1 hour

Room layout
Horse shoe

Resources required
- PowerPoint presentation: Training plan 17
- Software of trainer's choice to demonstrate how to film and produce a video.
- Training plan 17 supplementary information sheet: Creating a flipped learning professional development video (see page 209 and can be downloaded as a handout for participants)

Preparing the session

Ensure that you are confident in the skills of filming, creating and producing a video. Practise these beforehand and be very confident in your ability to demonstrate them to others.

Step-by-step guide to running the session

Phase	Timing	Format	Content
Introduction	5 mins	Presentation	• Brief recap on previous session about how a flipped learning approach to professional development can be extremely effective.
Activity 1	15 mins	Individual reflection followed by Think, Pair, Share	• Creating the content: o How long do you want your video to be? o Is there an optimum length? o Where are you going to film the video? o What do you want the video to achieve?
Activity 2	15 mins	Presentation and group discussion Demonstration	• How can you produce a video to share with your staff as part of their pre-learning? • What software can you use? • Demonstration of one or two types of simple methods of screencasting or video production.
Activity 3	20 mins	Individual task	• Plan the content for a pre-session video for an upcoming session that you might be delivering. • Discuss your plan with a fellow participant. Compare and contrast your approach to theirs.
Plenary and next steps	5 mins	Group discussion	• Recap the main points from the session. • Identify next steps for individuals as they move towards being ready to create their first flipped learning video. • Next steps tasks: o Watch some examples of pre-session learning videos that have been created for a flipped learning approach to professional development. o Take a look at Jon Tait's professional development videos on YouTube. Search for 'AGS Inspire: Leadership'.

Creating a flipped learning professional development video

How long should your video be?

We all like things in bitesize chunks. Try to keep your video down to under ten minutes. There is far more chance of people watching it all if it's in single figures.

Where should you film the video?

Film it anywhere where there are no distractions and it's quiet, preferably with a blank wall behind you. Take a quick test film and ask yourself if it looks and sounds professional.

What do you want the video to achieve?

A pre-session video that people watch prior to attending a flipped session should give the delegates all of the main information that they require. If it is effective, it means you don't have to cover this information in the session, meaning you have more time to do other things and make the session more practical. This lets delegates practise the skills they have learned in the video.

How to produce the video

Don't try to overcomplicate the video production. Keep it simple. Start by just speaking to your webcam. Once you get more skilled with video editing software, think about adding some keywords to the screen when you are talking about important factors. This way it will help people to focus on key points.

Tips on content

Try to be as concise as possible. Don't ramble on about non-essential things. This can add extra minutes to your video that you don't need. Get to the main points quickly and make them clearly and concisely.

How do people see the video?

Simply publish it to either YouTube or your internal network and then give out the link to everyone who has signed up to attend.

3   Evaluating professional development

As we have discussed previously in this section, there are many ways to create professional learning opportunities for the staff in your school. However, how do you know what impact these sessions are having on the development of your staff and, more importantly, the outcomes of your students?

You might think that putting on a range of different sessions, covering different topics and using innovative delivery styles is enough to suggest that your professional development programme is hitting the mark, but how do you know it's making a difference? After all, think about all of the human resource time that goes into the planning and delivery of your sessions – individual planning time, actual delivery time, how many people attend each session (multiplied by their approximate hourly rate). Once you begin to add all of this up, are you getting value for money from your programme? And if you believe that you are, what evidence are you using to judge this or form your opinion?

Given the time, effort and human resource cost that goes into professional development each year, it should be annually evaluated, just like any other intervention or school improvement strategy that you spend thousands of pounds on. However, in my experience of talking to senior leaders in schools up and down the country, this doesn't always seem to be the case. It may be that you are spending significant amounts of time and money on something that isn't having any impact at all.

How can you evaluate professional development?

Trying to put your finger on one specific strategy that has brought about school improvement is never an easy thing to do, but that doesn't mean that you shouldn't try. If you can begin to identify what is having the biggest impact in your school on student outcomes, then you can become far more strategic in your approach to school improvement. Instead of just doing more of the same and hoping it works, effective leaders perform a forensic analysis on all the strategies that they use and then do more of the strategies that are proven to increase student outcomes. The same should apply to professional development. Identify areas that you feel require development across the whole school or with individuals, put in place the CPD, then evaluate its impact. If it works, do more of it; if it doesn't, try to find out why before doing any more of it.

There are many ways to evaluate the impact of your professional development programme. Some of the following ways may work for some areas of professional development and not for others, and some may work in some contexts and, again, not in others. The ideas are not to be seen as an exhaustive list or a checklist of things you have to do in order to evaluate impact, but more a menu of strategies for you to choose from when judging whether your CPD strategies are having any impact. Some of these may complement others in order for you to use a range of evaluation strategies to build up a bigger picture of your programme's effectiveness.

Student outcomes

Ultimately, it's all about student outcomes. You can argue until the cows come home that your professional development programme is making your teachers more expert in their field and better classroom practitioners, but if student outcomes don't improve as a result of this, then your argument starts to hold no weight. Being able to track the improvement of student outcomes and headline school performance data against what you have done to improve the quality of teaching in the classroom is essential in any high-performing programme. It does, however, require you to go a little deeper into the analysis than you normally would go. For example, how can you judge if your session on 'Staff wellbeing' has had an impact on whole-school outcomes? If you can find some reliable data, then this is gold dust. Externally assessed student outcomes are the gold mark when it comes to evaluating the success of a strategy in school. You can have all the internal subjective data you want, but it is never as authentic and reliable as improved student outcomes.

External reports

As with student outcomes, any expert external judgement on the performance of the school should be sought after and seen as a very reliable indicator. Reports can be in the form of Ofsted reports, Local Authority whole-school or subject-specific reports, or even bespoke commissioned reports on a specific area of school performance. Within these reports you might be able to find evidence of where the report has praised an area that you have led professional development on, or where the report has identified a significant improvement in student outcomes due to a strategy that you have put in place. Collating a document containing all of these statements is a quick and easy way to refer back to them when required.

Lesson observations and learning walks

Apart from student outcomes in externally assessed examinations, one of the other obvious places to look for impact of your professional development sessions is in the classroom itself. If you have been working with individuals, groups or the whole staff on a certain teaching technique or strategy, go and look for it in their daily practice. If you think that your session on questioning went really well a few weeks ago, but then when you conduct a learning walk you don't see any visible signs of it in action, you need to question the impact that it had. The key with any strategy that you offer teachers as part of your professional development programme is whether it becomes embedded in daily routines. If it is only used for a couple of weeks whilst it's fresh in people's memories, then it's had no long-term impact and will therefore have no impact on student outcomes.

Work scrutiny

For some strategies, learning walks or lesson observations might not be an effective method of evaluating their impact. For these strategies, taking a longer, deeper look in student books can be the best way of telling if they're working. It is in student books that you can really see if strategies are embedded and having an impact over a period of time because they are clearly becoming part of the daily routines of both staff and students. If you believe that a strategy is now fully embedded, you should be able to see it throughout a selection of books and across a selection of subjects. Any inconsistencies will enable you to review its impact and inform you who needs to revisit this session.

Evaluation forms

On most external professional development courses I've ever been to, I've had to fill out a course evaluation form. On the form I've had to say how successful I thought the course was and if it had improved my practice as a result of me being there. But how often do you get your own staff to fill out these evaluation forms? Although this should never be thought of as being as reliable as external student outcomes, it may form part of a bigger picture of the quality and impact of your professional development programme. There are, however, two problems that people often run into when using session evaluation forms.

1. People aren't always truthful. If you ask someone to fill in a form in their own handwriting whilst they are sat in front of you, the chances are they won't tell you what they really thought of the session unless it was amazing.
2. Asking someone to tell you how good a training session was before they have had the chance to try it out in their own classroom over a period of time is hardly going to give you a reliable source of data when looking at whether it's improved the outcomes of your students.

A potential solution to this is to use an online survey tool, something like Survey Monkey. These online solutions let staff fill surveys in anonymously and also can be sent out at a later date, once staff have actually had the chance to try these strategies out. Due to their online nature, they can also analyse all of the data for you and immediately give you an indication of how successful a session has been, rather than you having to spend hours going through each form and creating your own analysis.

Blogging

An extension of the above idea on staff evaluation forms after they have tried the strategies in their classroom is for staff to blog about their experiences. Getting staff to write you a few paragraphs on the session they went to, how they have implemented it in their classroom and the impact it's had can be extremely powerful. Not only can it be shared with other staff, but it can also let the teacher writing the blog post see how their practice has changed as a result of attending the session. Sharing these blogs amongst the whole staff can also be a very powerful tool in your armoury. Anyone can bring in a blog post that they've read on Twitter from a school in another part of the world and say, 'Let's try this', but it's usually met with 'I bet they don't teach kids like ours'. Sharing blogs of what has worked with your kids, in your building and written by your staff, demonstrates that it is possible for everyone and removes any excuses.

Staff retention

Although not a strong and reliable indicator of the impact of your professional development programme, staff retention is a worthwhile indicator to add to the bigger picture. If teachers feel like the school professional development programme is making them into a better teacher and they feel good about their own personal and professional development, they are less likely to want to jump ship at the first opportunity. Take a look back through previous years with your HR team. How many teachers have been leaving each year on average? Has this changed since you implemented a new professional development system that is now both professional and truly develops people?

Cross-referencing with appraisal

Finally, if you have an effective staff appraisal system, it should talk to your professional development programme. Members of staff that have targets to improve certain aspects of their teaching should have these listed as one of their appraisal targets. If your programme is having the desired impact, then you should begin to see staff achieving these targets and this should be backed up by the evidence that we have already discussed – lesson observations, work scrutiny, student outcomes, etc. In turn, the topics you are delivering should also be informed by some of these targets. It is no good scratching your head because your professional development programme is not having any impact if it's not being targeted at the right areas in the first place.

Share your evaluations with staff

If you have already been evaluating the impact of your professional development programme, how often have you shared this with your staff? You might have some fantastic data to suggest that the sessions that the staff have been coming to have had a significant impact on the outcomes of the students. However, unless you share this with staff, you are missing a trick, as everyone likes to know that their efforts have led to improvements. If your staff know that the sessions they have been coming to are having a significant and noticeable impact on student outcomes, they are going to be far more likely to want to attend in the future, thus creating a self-motivating professional development programme for school improvement.

Bibliography

Aguilar, J. (2014) 'What makes a great school leader?', www.edutopia.org/blog/qualities-of-great-school-leader-elena-aguilar

Ainsworth, P. (2016) *Bloomsbury CPD Library: Middle Leadership*. London: Bloomsbury Education.

Ainsworth, P. (2018) '10 tips on how to run a mid-year appraisal', *Teacher Toolkit*, https://www.teachertoolkit.co.uk/2018/02/28/mid-year-appraisal/

Allison, S. (2014) *Perfect Teacher-Led CPD*. Carmarthen: Crown House Publishing.

Battelle for Kids (2016) '6 lessons for leading change in schools', https://www.battelleforkids.org/learning-hub/learning-hub-item/6-lessons-learned-about-leading-and-navigating-change-in-schools

Berry, J. (2014) '10 top tips for teachers heading into senior leadership teams', www.theguardian.com/teacher-network/teacher-blog/2014/aug/26/top-tips-teachers-school-senior-leadership-team

Bird, T. and Cassell, J. (2017) *The Leader's Guide to Presenting: How to use soft skills to get hard results*. Harlow: FT Publishing Ltd.

Blanchard, K. (2008) 'Leadership strategies for making change stick', https://resources.kenblanchard.com/whitepapers/leadership-strategies-for-making-change-stick

Buck, A. (2017) *Leadership Matters: How leaders at all levels can create great schools*. Woodbridge: John Catt Educational Ltd.

Carter, O. (2016) 'Visible leadership for better learning', Optimus Education, http://blog.optimus-education.com/visible-leadership-better-learning

Catapano, J. (2015) 'Relationship building with teacher colleagues', *TeachHUB*, http://www.teachhub.com/relationship-building-teacher-colleagues

Bibliography

Collins, J. (2001) *Good to Great*. London: Random House.

Cope, A. and Whittaker, A. (2014) *Be Brilliant Every Day*. Chichester: Capstone.

Cuddy, A. (2016) *Presence: Bringing your boldest self to your biggest challenges*. London: Orion.

DfE (2017) 'Data analysis: Teachers leaving the profession'.

Diffen LLC (2014) 'Accountability vs. responsibility', www.diffen.com/difference/Accountability_vs_Responsibility

Dunford, J. (2016) *The School Leadership Journey: What 40 years in education has taught me about leading schools in an ever-changing landscape*. Woodbridge: John Catt Educational Ltd.

Dweck, C. (2017) *Mindset: Changing the way you think to fulfil your potential*. (updated edn). New York, NY: Robinson.

Goddard, V. (2014) *The Best Job In The World*. Carmarthen: Crown House Publishing.

Grint, K. (2008) 'Wicked problems and clumsy solutions: The role of leadership', leadershipforchange.org.uk/wp-content/uploads/Keith-Grint-Wicked-Problems-handout.pdf

Headlee, C. (2015) TED Talk: '10 ways to have a better conversation', www.ted.com/talks/celeste_headlee_10_ways_to_have_a_better_conversation/up-next

Hilton, J. (2016) *Leading From the Edge: A school leader's guide to recognising and overcoming stress*. London: Bloomsbury Education.

Kell, E. (2018) *How to Survive in Teaching: Without imploding, exploding or walking away*. London: Bloomsbury Education.

Lemon, B. (2017) *Much Promise: Successful schools in England*. Woodbridge: John Catt Educational Ltd.

Levitin, D. (2015) TED Talk: 'How to stay calm when you know you'll be stressed', www.ted.com/talks/daniel_levitin_how_to_stay_calm_when_you_know_you_ll_be_stressed/up-next

Martinuzzi, B. (2013) '10 tips for managing difficult conversations', www.americanexpress.com/us/small-business/openforum/articles/ top-ten-tips-for-handling-the-difficult-conversation/

McCarthy, M. (2017) *Bloomsbury CPD Library: Mentoring and Coaching*. London: Bloomsbury Education.

McGill, R. M. (2014) '10 tips for tweeting teachers', www.teachertoolkit. co.uk/2014/08/01/10-tips-for-tweeting-teachers-by-teachertoolkit

McGill, R. M. (2015) *Teacher Toolkit: Helping you survive your first five years*. London: Bloomsbury Education.

McGill, R. M. (2017) '7 ways to manage difficult conversations', *Teacher Toolkit*, https://www.teachertoolkit.co.uk/2017/05/26/difficult-conversations/

Nicholls, D. (2016) 'Outstanding meetings: how groups drive improvement', https://dannicholls1.wordpress.com/2016/04/07/outstanding-meetings-how-can-groups-drive-improvement/

Ofsted (2017) School Inspection Handbook, www.gov.uk/government/ publications/school-inspection-handbook-from-september-2015

O'Keefe, B. (2011) '5 steps to better school/community collaboration', *Edutopia*, https://www.edutopia.org/blog/school-community-collaboration-brendan-okeefe

Peck, E. (2016) 'Why walking meetings can be better than sitting meetings', www. huffingtonpost.com/2015/04/09/walking-meetings-at-linke_n_7035258.html

Pink, D. (2011) *Drive*. New York, NY: Riverhead Books.

Povey, D. (2017) *Educating Drew: The real story of Harrop Fold School*. Woodbridge: John Catt Educational Ltd.

Rock, D. (2007) *Quiet Leadership: Six steps to transforming performance at work*. New York, NY: HarperCollins.

Sherrington, T. (2013) 'Great school leadership 2: vision', *Teacherhead*, https:// teacherhead.com/2013/09/13/great-leadership-2-vision/

Sherrington, T. (2016) 'Teacher turnover. Part of life.', *Teacherhead*, https:// teacherhead.creativeschools.co.uk/teacher-turnover-part-of-life/

Bibliography

Smith, S. (2017) 'Listen and learn. (Leading in stormy weather)', www.smithsmm.
wordpress.com/2017/12/28/listen-and-learn-leading-in-stormy-weather

Sobel, D. (2018) *Narrowing the Attainment Gap*. London: Bloomsbury Education.

Sutcliffe, J. (2012) 'How to build a winning team', www.theguardian.com/
teacher-network/2012/oct/08/top-tips-outstanding-school-leaders

Sutcliffe, J. (2013) *8 Qualities of Successful School Leaders*. London: Bloomsbury
Education.

Tait. J. (2014) 'Securing that leadership position', www.jontait.com/
securing-that-leadership-position/

TES (2008) 'Choose the right school', www.tes.com/articles/choose-right-school

Tierney, S. (2013a) 'What should we look for in senior leaders?', www.
leadinglearner.me/2013/05/12/what-should-we-look-for-in-senior-leaders

Tierney, S. (2013b) 'Preparing and applying for your first headship', www.
leadinglearner.me/2013/10/13/preparing-and-applying-for-your-first-headship/

Tierney, S. (2016) *Liminal Leadership: Building bridges across the chaos...because we
are standing on the edge*. Woodbridge: John Catt Educational Ltd.

Tomsett, J. (2018a) 'This much I know about... how, as school leaders, we have
to solve the recruitment crisis ourselves', www.johntomsett.com/2018/01/05/
this-much-i-know-about-how-as-school-leaders-we-have-to-solve-the-
recruitment-crisis-ourselves/

Tomsett, J. (2018b) 'From vision to action: establishing a vision for your school',
blog.optimus-education.com/vision-action-establishing-vision-your-school

Wiliam, D. (2012) 'Every teacher can improve', https://www.youtube.com/
watch?v=eqRcpA5rYTE

Index

Index